Mobile phones have increasingly become tools that consumers use for banking, payments, budgeting, and shopping. Given the rapid pace of developments in the area of mobile finance, the Federal Reserve Board began conducting annual surveys of consumers' use of mobile financial services in 2011. The survey examines trends in the adoption and use of mobile banking, payments, and shopping behavior and how the emergence of mobile financial services affects consumers' interaction with financial institutions.

This report presents findings from the 2014 survey, fielded in December, which focused on consumers' use of mobile technology to access financial services and make financial decisions. Where applicable, the findings from the current survey are also compared with the findings from the 2011, 2012, and 2013 surveys. Topics include consumer access to bank services using mobile phones ("mobile banking"), consumer payment for goods and services using mobile phones ("mobile payments"), and consumer shopping decisions facilitated by use of mobile phones. Details about the survey, its methodology, and limitations can be found in the body of the report and in a methodological appendix.

Key Findings

Key findings of the 2014 survey include:

- **Mobile phones are in widespread use.**

  —Eighty-seven percent of the U.S. adult population has a mobile phone, consistent with 2013.

  —Seventy-one percent of mobile phones are smartphones (Internet-enabled), up from 61 percent a year earlier.

- **The ubiquity of mobile phones is changing the way consumers access financial services.**

  —Thirty-nine percent of all mobile phone owners with a bank account have used mobile banking in the 12 months prior to the survey, up from 33 percent in 2013 and 29 percent in 2012.

  —Fifty-two percent of smartphone owners with a bank account have used mobile banking in the 12 months prior to the survey, up from 51 percent a year earlier.

  —Among those mobile phone users with bank accounts who do not currently use mobile banking, 11 percent think that they will probably or definitely use it within the next 12 months, down from 12 percent a year earlier.

  —The most common use of mobile banking is to check account balances or recent transactions (94 percent of mobile banking users).

  —Among mobile banking users, transferring money between an individual's own accounts (61 percent) and receiving an alert (e.g., a text message, push notification, or e-mail) from their bank (57 percent) are the second- and third-most common uses of mobile banking.

  —Fifty-one percent of mobile banking users have deposited a check using their mobile phone in the 12 months prior to the survey, up from 38 percent in 2013.

  —Among mobile banking users, the frequency of use has increased slightly, from a median of four times per month in 2013 to five times per month in 2014. This frequency was five times per month in 2012.

  —Residents of more rural areas have a lower incidence of mobile banking use than residents of more urban areas.

- **Mobile phones are also changing the way consumers make payments.**

  —Twenty-two percent of all mobile phone owners reported having made a mobile payment in the 12 months prior to the survey, up from 17 percent in 2013 and 15 percent in 2012.

—The share of smartphone users who reported having made a mobile payment in the 12 months prior to the survey has increased to 28 percent, up from 24 percent in both 2013 and 2012.

—Among mobile payment users with smartphones, the most common type of mobile payment was bill payment through an online system or mobile app (68 percent, up from 66 percent in 2013).

—Thirty-nine percent of all mobile payment users with smartphones have made a point-of-sale payment using their mobile phone in the 12 months prior to the survey, in line with the 39 percent reporting such payments in 2013.

—Of mobile payment users with smartphones who made point-of-sale mobile payments, 31 percent did so by scanning a barcode or QR code displayed on their phone's screen at check out (down from 39 percent in 2013), while 22 percent used an app that did not require tapping their mobile phone or scanning a barcode (up from 17 percent in 2013).

—Residents of more rural areas have a lower incidence of mobile payments use than residents of more urban areas.

• **A preference for other methods of banking and making payments, as well as concerns about security, continue to be the main impediments to the adoption of mobile financial services cited by some consumers.**

—Of those not using mobile banking, the primary reason respondents cited was a belief that their banking needs were being met without the use of mobile banking (86 percent).

—The primary reason non-mobile payment users gave for not using mobile payments was that they believe it is easier to pay with cash or credit/debit cards (75 percent).

—Concern about the security of the technology was a common reason given for not using mobile banking or mobile payments (62 percent and 59 percent, respectively, of non-users).

• **Smartphones are changing the way people shop and make financial decisions.**

—Forty-seven percent of smartphone users have comparison shopped with their phone while at a retail store, and 33 percent have used their phone to scan a product's barcode to find the best price for the item.

—Of those consumers who used their phones to comparison shop in a retail store, 69 percent have changed where they purchased a product as a result of the information they found.

—Forty-two percent of smartphone users have used their phone to browse product reviews or get product information while shopping at a retail store, and 79 percent of them changed the item they purchased based on this information.

—Sixty-three percent of mobile banking users have checked their account balance on their phone before making a large purchase in the previous 12 months leading up to the survey, and over half (53 percent) of them decided not to purchase an item as a result of their account balance or credit limit.

—Twenty-nine percent of all mobile phone users and 38 percent of smartphone users have used their phone to track purchases and expenses.

• **Mobile phones are prevalent among unbanked and underbanked consumers.**

—The share of consumers who are unbanked is 13 percent, and the share who are underbanked is 14 percent.

—Sixty-seven percent of the unbanked have access to a mobile phone, 65 percent of which are smartphones.

—Ninety percent of the underbanked have access to a mobile phone, 73 percent of which are smartphones.

—Forty-eight percent of underbanked consumers had used mobile banking in the 12 months prior to the survey.

In 2011, the Federal Reserve Board's Division of Consumer and Community Affairs conducted its first Survey of Consumers' Use of Mobile Financial Services. Since that time, the adoption of mobile financial services has continued to increase, along with the range of services offered. As part of its ongoing efforts to monitor developments in the mobile financial services arena and to gain insights into consumers' usage of, and attitudes toward, mobile financial services, the Board has continued to conduct the survey annually.[1] The fourth survey, conducted in December 2014, included a random sample of respondents to the previous survey in 2013, as well as a random sample of new respondents. The subsample of respondents who voluntarily completed both the 2013 and 2014 waves of the survey allows for the analysis of changes in behavior over the past year among these individuals.

Survey Background

The original survey instrument and subsequent waves of the survey were designed in consultation with a mobile financial services advisory group made up of key Federal Reserve System staff with relevant consumer research and payments backgrounds. The 2012, 2013, and 2014 survey samples were all composed of a mix of a randomly selected respondents to the previous year's survey and new survey respondents.

The 2014 survey was again administered by GfK, an online consumer research company, on behalf of the Board. The survey was conducted using a sample of adults ages 18 and over from KnowledgePanel®, a proprietary, probability-based web panel of more than 50,000 individuals from randomly sampled households; the sample was designed to be represen-

Table 1. Key survey response statistics: Main interview

	Number sampled for main survey	Qualified completes	Completion rate
2013 re-interviews	2,308	1,489	64.5%
Fresh cases	2,657	1,436	54.0%
Total primary sample	4,965	2,925	58.9%

tative of the U.S. population. After pretesting, the data collection for the survey began on December 5, 2014, and concluded on December 21, 2014.

For the results presented in the main body of this report, the sample was drawn following the method used for the 2012 and 2013 surveys. As shown in table 1, e-mails were sent to 2,308 randomly selected respondents to the 2013 survey and 2,657 randomly selected respondents from the remaining members of KnowledgePanel®. The respondents completed the survey in approximately 12 minutes (median time). Of the 2,925 respondents, 1,489 had responded to the 2013 survey one year before, while 1,436 were new survey respondents drawn from the general population.[2] Further details on the survey methodology are included in appendix 1.

As with any survey method, Internet panels can be subject to biases resulting from undercoverage or nonresponse and, in this case, potential underrepresentation of adults who may be uncomfortable with technology. Not everyone in the United States has access to the Internet, and there are demographic (income, education, age) and geographic (urban and rural) differences between those who do have access and those who do not. These concerns are addressed by GfK providing Internet access to respondents who

---

[1] See the "Consumers and Mobile Financial Services" reports series for previous years' survey findings. Results of the 2011, 2012, and 2013 surveys (published in March 2012, 2013, and 2014, respectively) are available at www.federalreserve.gov/communitydev/mobile_finance_publications.htm.

[2] The 2014 survey also included an oversample of respondents from rural areas. For comparability with prior years of the survey, the oversample was not used in computing the results in the main body of this report; therefore, respondents from the oversample are not included in table 1. However, selected statistics based on the oversample are included in box 1. Additional information on the sample is provided in appendix 1.

do not have it in order to include the portion of the population that does not have Internet access in KnowledgePanel®, and using sample weights to ensure that the Internet usage and key demographics of the sample population matches the adult U.S. population. See appendix 1 for a more detailed discussion. While care has been taken to ensure the survey results are generalizable to the adult U.S. population, the usual caveats regarding surveys nevertheless apply.

The full survey questionnaire is presented in appendix 2 and the responses to all the categorical survey questions are presented in appendix 3 in the order that the questions were asked of respondents. Tables of summary statistics for the respondent demographics by mobile phone usage are also included as tables C.66 to C.69. Beginning at table C.70, cross-tabulations are presented of consumers' use of mobile phones, mobile banking, and mobile payments by age, race, gender, education, and income.

The following sections of this report summarize key findings from the Federal Reserve Board's survey of consumers conducted by GfK, with a focus on how consumers use mobile phones to conduct their banking, make payments, enhance information gathering while shopping, and manage their finances. The numbers cited in this report are derived from the Board survey unless otherwise noted. All data were weighted to yield estimates for the U.S. adult population. Only questions pertaining to these topics are discussed in the report; however, the complete survey questionnaire and the results of the entire survey are summarized in appendix 2 and appendix 3.

Consumer Access to Mobile Phones

As of December 2014, 87 percent of the U.S. population ages 18 and above owned or had regular access to a mobile phone. While the percent of the adult population with mobile phones has remained constant over the previous two years, an increasing proportion of those own smartphones: this survey's 71 percent smartphone ownership rate among those with mobile phones is a substantial increase over the 61 percent rate reported in 2013,[3] 52 percent rate in 2012, and 44 percent rate in 2011.

Table 2. Smartphone usage by race/ethnicity
Percent, except as noted

Race/ethnicity	Smartphone usage			
	2011	2012	2013	2014
White, non-Hispanic	41	50	57	68
Black, non-Hispanic	47	54	63	66
Other, non-Hispanic	45	54	76	83
Hispanic	55	60	72	82
2+ races, non-Hispanic	43	59	64	65
Total	44	52	61	71
Number of respondents	2,002	2,291	2,341	2,603

Note: The denominator is all respondents with a mobile phone.

Rates of mobile phone usage remain high and consistent across demographic and socioeconomic groups. The prevalence of mobile phones demonstrates the extent to which they have become engrained in modern culture. Mobile phone usage is approximately 91 percent for persons ages 18 to 44, and declines only slightly to 87 percent for persons ages 45 to 59 and to 80 percent for persons ages 60 and over. Smartphone adoption is also higher among younger generations, with the differences being more pronounced among age groups: 84 percent of those ages 18 to 29 and 86 percent of those ages 30 to 44 who own a mobile phone have a smartphone, while 67 percent of mobile phone owners ages 45 to 59 and 47 percent of mobile phone owners ages 60 and over have a smartphone.

Mobile phone ownership varies slightly by race and ethnicity, with non-Hispanic whites, Hispanics, and non-Hispanic blacks having rates of 88 percent, 85 percent, and 83 percent, respectively. However, adoption of smartphones varies in a somewhat more pronounced way: 82 percent of Hispanic mobile phone users have a smartphone, compared to 68 percent of non-Hispanic whites and 66 percent of non-Hispanic blacks (table 2).

---

[3]   Throughout this report, percentages are calculated as a share of all those who were asked a question, including those who did not respond. Results on phone ownership from the Board's 2013 survey are very similar to those from the Pew Research Center for that year. In the June 2013 *Smartphone Ownership—*

2013 Update, the Pew Research Center reported that 91 percent of U.S. adults owned a mobile phone and 61 percent of adults with a mobile phone (or 56 percent of adults overall) had a smartphone. (See http://pewinternet.org/~/media//Files/Reports/2013/PIP_Smartphone_adoption_2013_PDF.pdf.) The 2013 Federal Deposit Insurance Corporation (FDIC) Survey of Unbanked and Underbanked Households provides measures of mobile and smartphone access at the household level. In 2013, its estimates showed that 83 percent of households owned or had regular access to a mobile phone and 67 percent of households with a mobile phone (or 56 percent of households overall) had a smartphone. (See www.fdic.gov/householdsurvey/2013report.pdf.)

Mobile phone and smartphone usage does vary with the level of household income. In households earning less than $25,000 per year, 74 percent of adults have a mobile phone of some type, and 53 percent have a smartphone. Use of both mobile phones and smartphones increases with income, reaching 95 percent and 85 percent, respectively, for adults in households earning more than $100,000 per year.

The relatively high prevalence of mobile phone and smartphone use among younger generations, minorities, and those with low levels of income—groups that are more likely to be unbanked or underbanked—makes mobile phones a potential platform for expanding financial access and inclusion.

In 2014, the share of consumers who were unbanked rose to 13 percent from 10 percent in 2013.[4] The share of consumers who would be described as underbanked—defined as having a bank account but also using an alternative financial service such as a money order, check cashing service, pawn shop loan, auto title loan, paycheck advance/deposit advance, or a payday loan—was 14 percent in 2014.[5]

Among individuals who are unbanked, 67 percent have access to a mobile phone and 65 percent of these are smartphones. Smartphone ownership has been increasing among the unbanked. The share of the unbanked with access to a mobile phone was 69 percent in 2013 and 59 percent in 2012, approximately half of which were smartphones.

Among the underbanked, 90 percent have a mobile phone, 73 percent of which are smartphones. Further, 48 percent of the underbanked with mobile phones reported using mobile banking in the 12 months prior to the survey, while 32 percent reported making mobile payments.

Trends in the Utilization of Mobile Banking and Payments

Services that allow consumers to obtain financial account information and conduct transactions with their financial institution ("mobile banking") and that allow consumers to make payments, transfer money, or pay for goods and services ("mobile payments") have become increasingly prevalent. Over the past several years, these services have become available at a broader range of institutions and the types of services continue to evolve. With increased dissemination of technology and a broadening array of options, consumer adoption of mobile financial services has risen. In the 2011 survey, for instance, 22 percent of mobile phone users with bank accounts and 43 percent of smartphone users with bank accounts reported that they had used mobile banking in the previous 12 months.[6] These proportions have increased in each year of the survey. In the 2014 survey, the prevalence of mobile banking continued to increase, reaching 39 percent of mobile phone users with bank accounts and 52 percent of smartphone users with bank accounts (figure 1).

Use of mobile payments has also increased. In 2011, 12 percent of mobile phone users and 23 percent of smartphone users reported using mobile payments. By 2014, usage of mobile payments had increased to 22 percent for mobile phone users and increased to 28 percent for smartphone users. The steady increases in the adoption rate among all mobile phone users, but more gradual rise in the adoption rate among smartphone users, suggest that smartphone adoption substantially contributed to the increased use of mobile payments.

A continuing impediment to adoption of either mobile banking or mobile payments appears to be consumers' limited demand for them: many consumers said their needs were already being met without mobile banking or payments, that they were comfortable with non-mobile options, and that they did not see a clear benefit from using either service. In addition, around one in five (22 percent) of those with mobile phones and bank accounts indicated they do

---

[4] In 2011 and 2012, the wording of the bank account question was "Do you or does your spouse/partner currently have a checking, savings, or money market account?" In 2013 and 2014, the wording of the bank account question changed slightly from the prior years to explicitly reference "bank or credit union" accounts: "Do you or does your spouse/partner currently have some type of bank or credit union account such as a checking, savings, or money market account?"

[5] Due to changes in the way this question was asked, the 2014 figures for underbanked households may not be comparable to results from earlier years. Most notably, relative to the 2013 report, "money order" was added to the list of alternative financial services used by underbanked households, and "payroll card" was removed.

[6] Here, the figures for mobile banking in the 2011 survey are expressed as percentages of mobile phone users with bank accounts. These figures differ slightly from those published in the 2011 report, which were calculated as a percent of all mobile phone users. Similarly, other estimates in the text may differ from the figures presented in appendix 3 or from estimates published in earlier reports because a subsample of the respondents was used for the calculation.

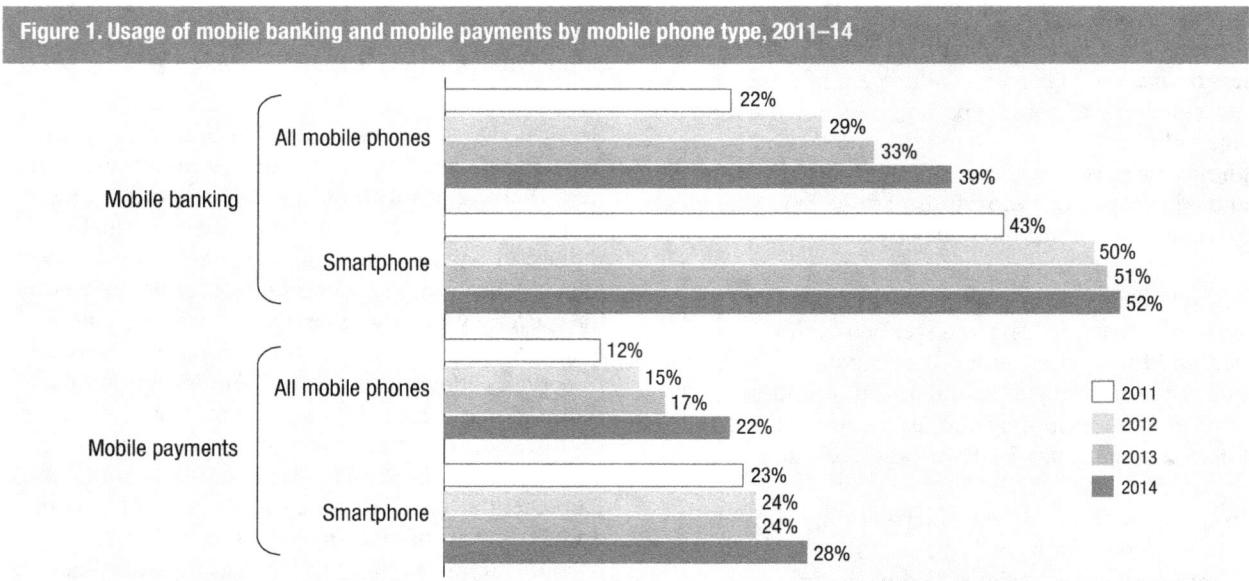

Figure 1. Usage of mobile banking and mobile payments by mobile phone type, 2011–14

Note: For mobile banking, the results are derived from respondents with bank accounts and mobile phones and all respondents with bank accounts and smartphones, respectively. For mobile payments, the results are derived from respondents with mobile phones and all respondents with smartphones, respectively.

not know if their bank or credit union offers mobile banking, which may be consistent with a lack of interest in these services among a portion of the population. That said, the share who do not know if mobile banking is available from their bank decreased from 28 percent in the 2013 survey, and the share that said their bank does not offer the service decreased as well—from 6 percent in 2013 to 4 percent in 2014. These results suggest an increase in availability and consumer awareness of mobile banking services.

Concerns about the security of mobile banking and mobile payment technologies are also frequently

cited as reasons why consumers chose not to adopt these technologies. Consumers appear to be more cognizant of the need to protect the personal information stored on their phones, as they are increasingly using passwords to protect their smartphones. The share of smartphone owners who password protect their phone increased to 69 percent in 2014, from 61 percent in 2013 and 54 percent in 2012.[7]

---

[7] At least one major mobile phone operating system has changed its default settings to require users to set a password unless they opt out. This change in default setting could also increase the incidence of password protection.

Box 1. Use of Mobile Financial Services among Rural Respondents

Mobile financial services may offer convenience or access in different ways to different subpopulations. One group that could especially benefit from mobile services is rural residents. Because rural residents may have to travel longer distances to visit financial institutions compared to urban consumers, mobile banking services may be particularly convenient. However, there are also countervailing factors that could make usage less likely. To learn more, the 2014 survey included an oversample of residents in rural areas.

Thirty-three percent of residents in non-metropolitan (non-metro) areas reported using mobile banking services in the prior 12 months, compared with 39 percent of respondents in metropolitan (metro) areas. Similarly, a smaller percentage (17 percent) of non-metro respondents reported using mobile payments in the prior 12 months relative to respondents in metro areas (23 percent).

This commonly used metropolitan/non-metropolitan distinction, however, has some limitations as a way to identify rural areas. In particular, non-metro areas include some places that are connected to urbanized areas and have a diversity of access to financial services. To provide an alternate measure of usage of mobile financial services for rural respondents, the survey results were also analyzed using a more narrow definition, measuring as "remote areas" only the respondents who live in small towns and rural areas with low commuting flows to urban places.[1] Fairly similar patterns persisted using this definition: 32 percent used mobile banking in remote rural areas, compared to 39 percent for everyone else, and 20 percent of those from remote rural areas used mobile payments, compared to 22 percent of the rest of respondents (figure A).

If, by either measure, rural residents appear to use mobile financial services at least somewhat less than those in non-rural areas, why would this be?

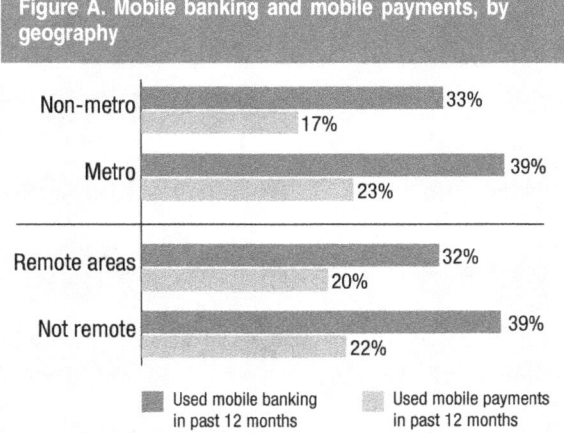

Figure A. Mobile banking and mobile payments, by geography

Non-metro: 33% (Used mobile banking in past 12 months), 17% (Used mobile payments in past 12 months)
Metro: 39%, 23%
Remote areas: 32%, 20%
Not remote: 39%, 22%

■ Used mobile banking in past 12 months   ■ Used mobile payments in past 12 months

Results from this survey point to some combination of differing technology, access to broadband services, services offered by financial institutions, and consumer awareness of those services.

Non-metro residents are slightly less likely than metro residents—84 versus 88 percent—to own a mobile phone, but considerably less likely to own a smartphone—54 versus 63 percent. They are also less likely to report near-constant access. When asked to characterize their Internet access on a mobile phone through wifi or a wireless network, 57 percent of non-metro respondents described it as "nearly always available," compared to 64 percent of respondents in metro areas (table A).[2] This relative lack of smartphone ownership and constant mobile Internet access may make use of certain mobile services less attractive or perhaps not possible.

When it comes to mobile banking, the supply of services also appears to differ. When asked whether mobile banking was offered by their financial institution, 65 percent of respondents in non-metro areas said yes, compared to 75 percent in metro areas (figure B). A higher share (30 percent) of respondents in non-metro areas also reported not knowing if mobile banking was offered by their financial institution, compared to 21 percent in urban areas. Whether this represents a lack of interest by rural consumers or simply a lack of awareness, it would seem that fewer rural residents have access to

(continued on next page)

---

[1] This alternate measure uses Rural-Urban Commuting Area (RUCA) codes, developed by the Department of Agriculture. The "Remote areas" correspond to small towns (less than 2,500 people) and rural areas with low urban commuting in RUCA code categories 7.0, 7.2, 8.0, 8.2, 9.0, 10.0, 10.2, and 10.3. (See www.ers.usda.gov/data-products/rural-urban-commuting-area-codes.aspx.) The companion category "Not remote" includes most portions of metropolitan and micropolitan areas, as well as small towns and rural areas that have a substantial secondary commuting flow (30–50 percent) to urban areas. This narrower definition of rural areas is very similar to a definition developed by the WWAMI Rural Health Research Center (http://depts.washington.edu/uwruca/ruca-maps.php). See appendix 1 for additional information on the sampling methods used for the primary sample and rural oversample included in this analysis.

[2] Nearly 1.3 million people in rural areas lacked access to mobile broadband in 2012, and rural residents generally face greater challenges with mobile coverage than urban residents. See https://apps.fcc.gov/edocs_public/attachmatch/FCC-13-34A1.pdf.

Box 1. Use of Mobile Financial Services among Rural Respondents–*continued*

Table A. Internet access on mobile phone through wifi or a wireless network (3G, 4G, LTE) is...

	Almost always available	Not always available, but is available at convenient locations	Available only at locations that require extra effort or planning to get to	Not available	I do not need access to the Internet on my mobile phone
Non-metro	57%	12%	2%	10%	20%
Metro	64%	8%	1%	7%	18%
Remote areas	59%	10%	1%	10%	19%
Not remote	63%	9%	1%	8%	18%

Note: Here and elsewhere in this report, totals may not add to 100 percent due to rounding and question non-response.

Figure B. Bank or credit union offers mobile banking, by geography

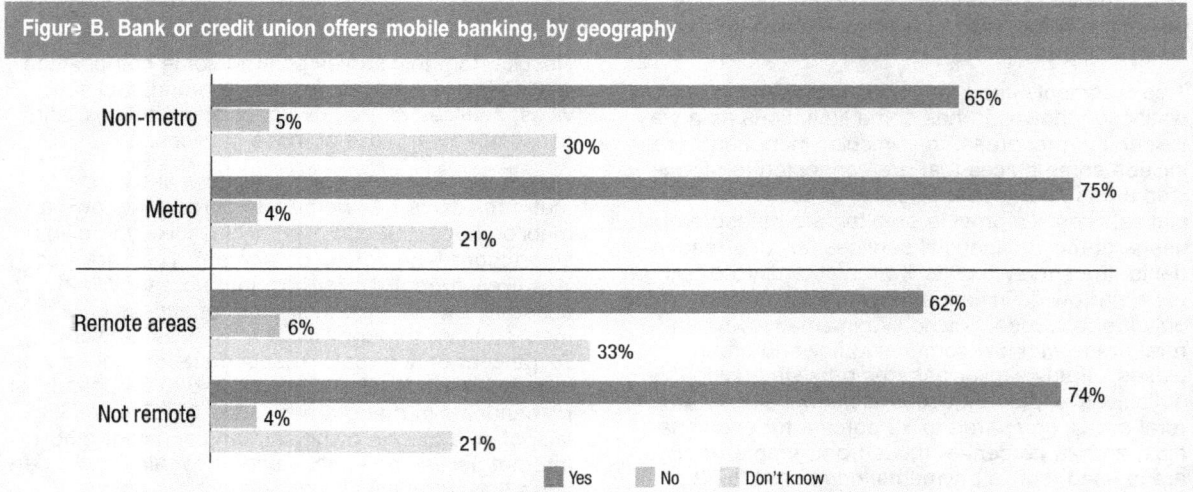

	Yes	No	Don't know
Non-metro	65%	5%	30%
Metro	75%	4%	21%
Remote areas	62%	6%	33%
Not remote	74%	4%	21%

mobile banking or are aware of available mobile banking services relative to residents of more urban areas.

Demographic differences between residents of metro and non-metro areas also may be a factor in any observed differences in the use of technology or the adoption of mobile financial services across areas.[3] In addition, preferences regarding technology use may be correlated with residential location apart from these other demographic factors.

Overall, respondents from non-metro areas are as likely to be "banked" as metro area respondents—86 versus 87 percent, respectively—but somewhat less likely to use either mobile banking services or mobile payments. The lower usages may be associated with lower availability of or consumers' knowledge about mobile banking services by their financial institution, lower levels of smartphone adoption, and less continuous mobile broadband access. They could also be attributed to other factors, including differences between urban and rural residents in preferences, demographic characteristics, or demand for these services. These results indicate that the promise of mobile technology as a way to bridge some challenges of living in rural areas may have not yet been fully realized.

---

[3] For example, estimates from the 2013 American Community Survey show that the median age of the population in non-metro areas is higher than in metro areas. Mobile banking use is lower among older consumers, as noted in this report.

Survey respondents were given a set of screening questions that asked if they had access to a bank account, the Internet, and a mobile phone. They were further asked about the various ways in which they access their financial accounts. Of the 87 percent of American consumers who have a checking, savings, or money market account, the majority use some form of technology to interact with their financial institution.

As shown in figure 2, the most common way of interacting with a financial institution remains in-person at a branch, with 87 percent of consumers who have a bank account reporting that they had visited a branch and spoken with a teller in the 12 months prior to the survey. The second-most common means of access in the previous 12 months was

using an automated teller machine (ATM) at 75 percent, followed by online banking at 74 percent.[8] One-third of all consumers with bank accounts used telephone banking, while 35 percent used mobile banking, up from 30 percent the previous year.[9] (For

[8] The definition of online banking changed slightly between the 2012 and 2013 surveys. For the 2011 and 2012 surveys the definition was "Online banking involves checking your account balance and recent transactions, transferring money, paying bills, or conducting other related transactions with your bank or credit card company using the Internet." For the 2013 and 2014 surveys, the definition was "Online banking involves checking your account balance and recent transactions, transferring money, paying bills, or conducting other related transactions with your bank or credit union using the Internet."

[9] The relative prevalence of channel usage in the Board's Mobile Survey is similar to results from the 2013 FDIC Survey of Unbanked and Underbanked Households. Of the households with bank accounts that reported accessing their accounts in the

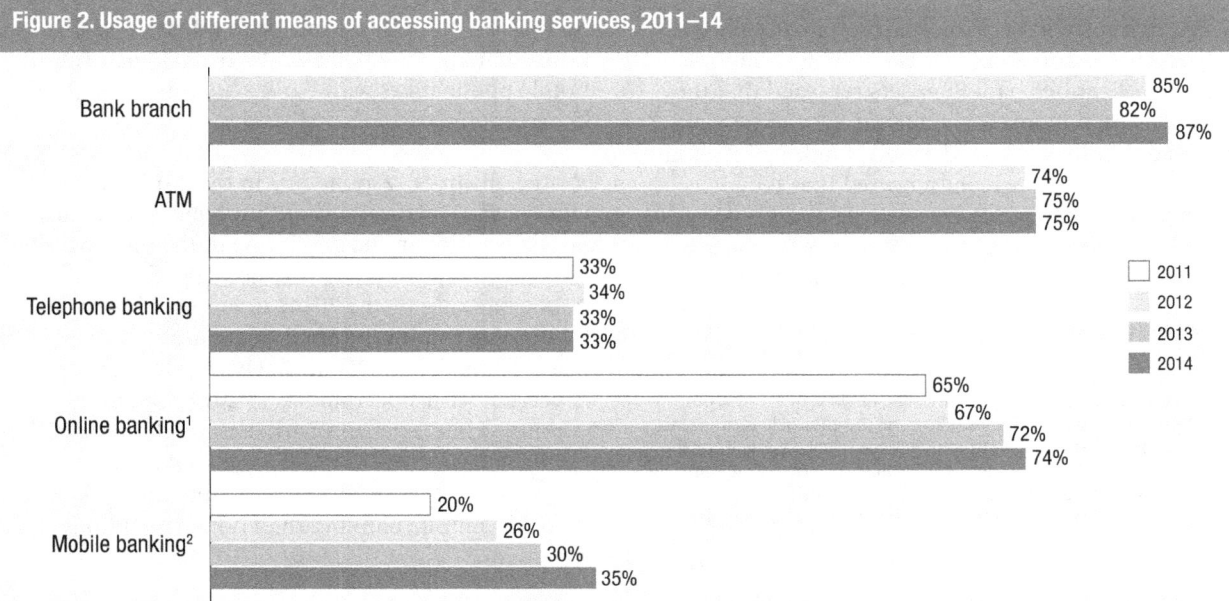

Figure 2. Usage of different means of accessing banking services, 2011–14

Note: Percentages are of all respondents with a checking, savings, or money market account for each banking channel, regardless of mobile phone ownership or access to the Internet. Questions about usage of bank branches and ATMs were not included on the 2011 survey.

1. For online banking, respondents who reported that they did not have regular access to the Internet other than that provided by GfK were not asked the online banking question in the 2011–2013 surveys. In the 2014 survey, all respondents with bank accounts were asked the question about online banking, which raised the measure for 2014 to 74 percent—2 percentage points higher than if these respondents had been excluded as in prior years.

2. For mobile banking, the percentages here may differ from the incidence rates elsewhere in this report because the latter are computed for those with mobile phones and bank accounts.

additional information on the use of various banking channels by mobile banking users, see box 2.)

Mobile Banking

The Federal Reserve survey defines mobile banking as "using a mobile phone to access your bank or credit union account. This can be done either by accessing your bank or credit union's web page through the web browser on your mobile phone, via text messaging, or by using an app downloaded to your mobile phone."[10]

Adoption Rates

The adoption of mobile banking has continued to increase in the past year. When asked about usage in the previous 12 months, 39 percent of mobile phone users with a bank account reported that they used mobile banking, a proportion that has been steadily climbing (figure 1). Mobile banking among smartphone users with a bank account is substantially higher at 52 percent, up modestly from earlier surveys. The higher incidence of mobile banking adoption among smartphone users suggests that as smartphone adoption continues to increase, mobile banking usage may also increase.

A significant fraction of mobile banking users have only recently adopted the technology. Although the majority of mobile banking users reported that they started using it more than one year ago, 15 percent reported that they adopted mobile banking in the last six months, and 12 percent reported that they adopted mobile banking between six and twelve months ago. Among those consumers with mobile phones who do not currently use mobile banking,

11 percent reported that they will "probably" or "definitely" use mobile banking in the following 12 months.

Although previous surveys suggest that the reported adoption intentions of the respondents do not perfectly reflect subsequent behavior, there is an association between the planned use of mobile banking and subsequent adoption. Using the panel of respondents to both the 2013 and 2014 Board surveys, it is possible to compare the reported mobile banking adoption intention over the next 12 months from the 2013 survey to the reported use of mobile banking in the 2014 survey. Of those consumers who reported in 2013 that they would "definitely" or "probably" adopt mobile banking in the following 12 months, only 28 percent had, in fact, adopted mobile banking one year later. Nonetheless, this is a higher proportion than those who said they did not expect their activity to change. Among those who indicated that they "probably will not" and "definitely will not" adopt mobile banking, 15 percent and 2 percent, respectively, had adopted mobile banking in 2014.

In total, 11 percent of those who reported that they were not mobile banking users in 2013 reported being mobile banking users in 2014.[11] However, 14 percent of those who were mobile banking users in 2013 reported that they had not used mobile banking in 2014.[12] Among panel respondents overall, mobile banking usage increased from 33 percent of mobile phone users with bank accounts in 2013 to 35 percent in 2014.

For the group of respondents in the 2013 survey who believed they "definitely" or "probably" would use mobile banking in the coming year, the most notable difference between those who actually did adopt mobile banking by the 2014 survey and those who did not was that the adopters were more likely to own a smartphone. Of this likely-to-adopt group, 42 percent with smartphones in 2014 used mobile banking, while 3 percent with feature phones used mobile banking. In both the panel and cross-sectional data, smartphone users were more likely to engage in mobile banking than non-smartphone users.

In every year of the survey, older consumers have consistently been less likely to use mobile banking

---

previous 12 months, 79 percent used a bank teller; 70 percent used an ATM/kiosk; 55 percent used online banking; 26 percent used telephone banking; and 23 percent used mobile banking. Comparing these FDIC figures to the results from the 2013 Mobile Survey, the relative ranking of the channels is the same across the two surveys, but the incidence of use is higher in the Mobile Survey for all channels. The incidence of online banking and of households with Internet access are notably higher in the 2013 Mobile Survey than in the FDIC survey. This may be due to differences in the survey methodology. The FDIC survey is conducted by phone and in person. The Mobile Survey is conducted via an online panel.

[10] The definition of mobile banking in the 2011 and 2012 surveys differed slightly from the definition above. In the earlier surveys, mobile banking was defined as using "a mobile phone to access your bank account, credit card account, or other financial account. This can be done either by accessing your bank's web page through the web browser on your mobile phone, via text messaging, or by using an application downloaded to your mobile phone."

---

[11] This group represents 6 percent of panel respondents who were mobile phone users in both years.

[12] This group represents 4 percent of panel respondents who were mobile phone users in both years.

Box 2. Channel Use among Mobile Banking Users

Mobile banking can provide convenient access to some banking services. However, consumers may still need or want to use other banking channels. For example, a visit to an automated teller machine (ATM) or branch may be necessary to withdraw cash, and visiting a branch or talking with a customer service representative may be preferred ways of resolving a problem. Respondents to the survey were asked about their use of five banking channels (branch, ATM, telephone, online banking, and mobile banking), and the answers provide a fuller picture of how mobile banking users interact with their bank or credit union.

Users of mobile banking services generally access them frequently, but not to the exclusion of other kinds of bank services. In general, mobile banking users reported using multiple channels to conduct banking business: 82 percent reported using four or five of these channels; only 2 percent used one or two channels. In the prior 12 months, 95 percent of mobile banking users also used online banking, 92 percent used an ATM, 85 percent visited a branch and spoke with a teller, and 36 percent used telephone banking (table A).

Most mobile banking users (90 percent) reported accessing mobile banking in the preceding month, and the median number of uses for those who used it in that month was five. Similarly, among mobile banking users who accessed online banking, 97 percent used online banking in the prior month,

and the median number of uses of online banking was six. The FDIC has noted that many banks have required their customers to be enrolled in online banking before they can enroll in mobile banking, and some mobile banking features, such as setting up payees for bill payment and enrolling in alerts, may require an online setup.[1] These types of bank policies would contribute to the high level of online banking use we observed among mobile banking users. For mobile banking users who accessed ATMs and bank branches, the likelihood of having used those channels in the past month was lower (85 and 72 percent, respectively), and the median number of uses was lower as well (three for ATM and two for branch). These responses suggest that many mobile banking users use online and mobile banking quite consistently for their banking needs, and access other bank channels on a periodic basis.

In a separate question, respondents were asked to rank the three main ways they interact with their bank or credit union. Twenty-one percent of mobile banking users ranked the mobile channel first—a lower share than those who chose online banking (35 percent) or ATM (30 percent), but a higher share than for the branch (13 percent) or telephone banking (1 percent).[2] Tallying the share of mobile banking users who ranked each of the channels in their top three, the ATM channel had the largest share (80 percent), followed by online banking (73 percent), mobile banking (60 percent), branch (56 percent), and telephone banking (17 percent).

Taken together, these estimates indicate that while mobile banking users are utilizing technological platforms at a high rate and on a consistent basis, they have also maintained connections to their banks through the more traditional branch and ATM channels.

Table A. Channel access among mobile banking users
Percent, except as noted

	MB users who used channel in the past 12 months	MB users who used channel in the past month[1]	Median frequency of channel use past month[2]
Mobile banking	100	90	5
Online banking	95	97	6
ATM	92	85	3
Branch/teller	85	72	2
Telephone banking	36	68	2

[1] Of those who used channel in the past 12 months.

[2] Of those who used channel in the past month.

[1] For the full FDIC white paper "Assessing the Economic Inclusion Potential of Mobile Financial Services," see www.fdic.gov/ consumers/community/mobile/Mobile-Financial-Services.pdf.

[2] The 2013 FDIC National Survey of Unbanked and Underbanked Households reported the primary banking method for households who used mobile banking and accessed their account in the last 12 months as follows: online banking (50 percent), mobile banking (25 percent), ATM/Kiosk (15 percent), bank teller (7 percent), and telephone banking (2 percent). For the full report on the survey, see www.economicinclusion.gov/surveys/ 2013household/documents/2013_FDIC_Unbanked_HH_Survey_ Report.pdf.

than have younger consumers (table 3). For those with a mobile phone and a bank account, results from the 2014 survey indicate that mobile banking use is 60 percent for those in the 18-to-29 age range and 54 percent for those in the 30-to-44 age group. By comparison, only 13 percent of individuals ages

60 or older reported having used mobile banking. Usage has generally increased from year to year for all age groups.

Consistent with the data from previous surveys, minorities continue to be more likely to use mobile

Table 3. Use of mobile banking in past 12 months by age

Percent, except as noted

Age group	2011	2012	2013	2014
18–29	45	54	63	60
30–44	29	37	43	54
45–59	12	21	25	32
60+	5	10	9	13
Total	22	29	33	39
Number of respondents	1,859	2,180	2,187	2,437

Note: Percentages are of those in each group who have a mobile phone and a bank account.

Table 4. Use of mobile banking in the past 12 months by race/ethnicity

Percent, except as noted

Race/ethnicity	2011	2012	2013	2014
White, non-Hispanic	19	26	30	34
Black, non-Hispanic	35	39	42	43
Other, non-Hispanic	23	31	35	48
Hispanic	29	36	45	53
2+ races, non-Hispanic	21	36	31	41
Total	22	29	33	39
Number of respondents	1,859	2,180	2,187	2,437

Note: Percentages are of those in each group who have a mobile phone and a bank account.

banking than non-Hispanic whites. In particular, Hispanic mobile phone users with bank accounts show a higher rate of use of mobile banking (53 percent) relative to mobile phone users with bank accounts overall (39 percent) (table 4).

Among those with a mobile phone and bank account, mobile banking use is more common for those with higher levels of education. Usage for those with a college degree or some college (44 percent) is greater than for those with a high school degree or less (29 percent). In addition, mobile banking usage for those mobile phone users with bank accounts with household incomes of $40,000 and above (41 percent) is greater than for those with incomes below $40,000 (34 percent).

Common Mobile Banking Activities

Among those who reported using mobile banking in 2014, the most common mobile banking activity was checking financial account balances or transaction inquiries, with 94 percent of mobile banking users hav-

ing performed this function in the 12 months prior to the survey (figure 3). This was followed by transferring money between accounts, performed by 61 percent of users. In addition, 57 percent of mobile banking users received an alert from their financial institution through a text message, push notification, or e-mail. Depositing a check to an account electronically using a mobile phone camera (known as remote deposit capture) and making an online bill payment from a bank account using a mobile phone were the next most common activities (done by 51 percent and 48 percent of mobile banking users, respectively). Mobile banking users appear to be using mobile applications to conduct their banking transactions, as 71 percent of mobile banking users have installed their bank's application on their phones.

Among all mobile banking users, the frequency of mobile banking use has increased slightly over the past year. The median reported usage increased from four times per month in 2013 to five times per month

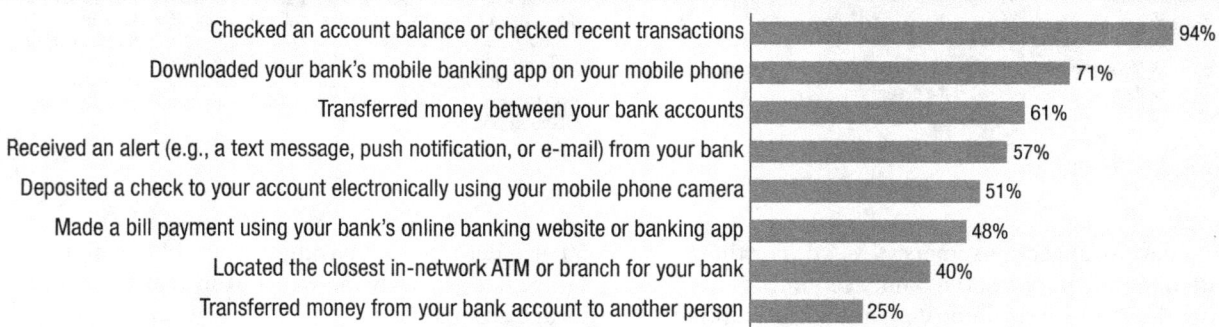

Figure 3. Using your mobile phone, have you done each of these in the past 12 months? (Among mobile banking users)

Checked an account balance or checked recent transactions — 94%
Downloaded your bank's mobile banking app on your mobile phone — 71%
Transferred money between your bank accounts — 61%
Received an alert (e.g., a text message, push notification, or e-mail) from your bank — 57%
Deposited a check to your account electronically using your mobile phone camera — 51%
Made a bill payment using your bank's online banking website or banking app — 48%
Located the closest in-network ATM or branch for your bank — 40%
Transferred money from your bank account to another person — 25%

Note: The number of respondents who were mobile banking users was 829.

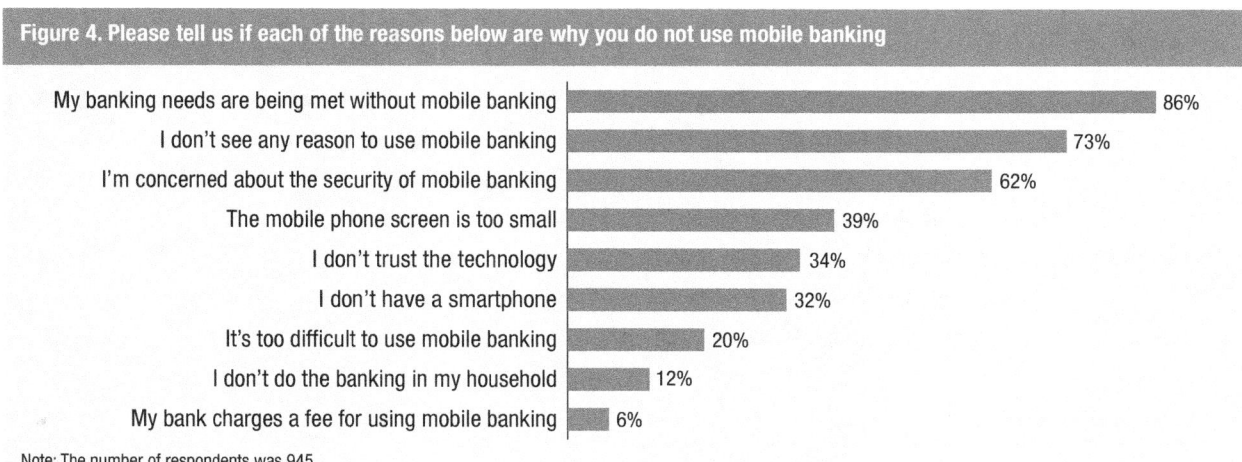

Figure 4. Please tell us if each of the reasons below are why you do not use mobile banking

My banking needs are being met without mobile banking	86%
I don't see any reason to use mobile banking	73%
I'm concerned about the security of mobile banking	62%
The mobile phone screen is too small	39%
I don't trust the technology	34%
I don't have a smartphone	32%
It's too difficult to use mobile banking	20%
I don't do the banking in my household	12%
My bank charges a fee for using mobile banking	6%

Note: The number of respondents was 945.

in 2014. Median usage for those with bank accounts who reported using mobile banking in 2011 and 2012 was also five times per month.

Among mobile bankers, there is variation in how frequently people use mobile banking services, and what types of activities they engage in. A relatively small share of mobile bankers (6 percent) indicated that they had used mobile banking in the previous year but had not used mobile banking in the previous month. These low-intensity users have a lower likelihood of engaging in all types of mobile banking activities, relative to mobile banking users overall. Like all mobile banking users, the most common task for low-intensity users is checking account balances or recent transactions (84 percent). Forty-three percent of the low-intensity users have downloaded their bank's mobile banking app—a sizeable share, but lower than the 71 percent of all mobile banking users who have done so. A greater proportion of low-intensity mobile banking users are non-Hispanic white (78 percent) compared to all mobile banking users (62 percent). Further, a greater proportion of low-intensity mobile banking users are ages 45 or older (49 percent), relative to all mobile banking users (31 percent).

In contrast, high-intensity users—defined here as mobile banking users who have conducted mobile banking tasks more than 10 times during the month prior to the 2014 survey—tend to conduct all mobile banking tasks at the same or higher rates than the larger group.[13] In particular, high-intensity users

reported making bill payments using their bank's online banking website or banking app and transferring money between their own accounts at higher rates than all mobile banking users. Overall, high-intensity users are demographically similar to the larger group of mobile banking users but include slightly greater shares of younger and black or Hispanic mobile banking users.

Reasons for Using—or Not Using—Mobile Banking

Convenience continues to be the most common reason consumers give for adopting mobile banking. Indeed, 35 percent of consumers indicated that the convenience was the main reason they started using mobile banking. Thirty-three percent of consumers said getting a smartphone was the main reason for using mobile banking. A further 20 percent of consumers indicated that the timing of their adoption of mobile banking was driven by their bank starting to offer the service.

Among those consumers with mobile phones and bank accounts who do not currently use mobile banking, several reasons for not using the service predominated—namely, they believed that their banking needs were being met without mobile banking (86 percent), they did not see any reason to use mobile banking (73 percent), and they were concerned about security (62 percent) (figure 4). The small size of the mobile phone screen was cited by 39 percent of consumers as the reason they do not

---

[13] For the purposes of this report, "high-intensity" users are identified as those respondents who have used mobile banking within the year prior to the 2014 survey and have used mobile banking more frequently than 75 percent of all mobile banking users, which corresponds to a frequency greater than 10 times in the month prior to the 2014 survey. Based on this definition, high-intensity users represent 22 percent of mobile banking users in the 2014 survey.

Figure 5. Which one of the following security aspects are you most concerned with?

All of the stated reasons	43%
Someone intercepting my data	22%
My phone getting hacked	17%
Losing my phone or having my phone stolen	9%
Someone using my phone without permission to access my account	4%
Companies misusing my personal information	2%
Malware or viruses being installed on my phone	2%
Other	0%

Note: The number of respondents was 600.

use mobile banking. This was followed by a lack of trust in the technology (34 percent) and not having a smartphone (32 percent) as reasons for not using mobile banking. Less commonly cited reasons included the difficulty associated with using mobile banking (20 percent) and not doing the banking in the household (12 percent). The incidence of reasons for not using mobile banking was generally consistent between the 2013 and 2014 surveys. However, in the 2014 survey, concerns about the security of mobile banking decreased from 69 percent in 2013. Also, fewer respondents reported that the small size of the mobile phone screen (44 percent in 2013) and not having a smartphone (44 percent in 2013) were reasons why they had not used mobile banking.

Consumers who expressed concerns about the security of mobile banking were asked to specify what aspect was of greatest concern (figure 5). Some reported fears of data interception (22 percent), phone "hacking" (17 percent), and lost or stolen phones (9 percent). While additional specific concerns were noted by small numbers of respondents, the most common response was that they were concerned with all of those security risks occurring (43 percent).

When consumers who do not use mobile banking were asked what mobile banking activities they would be interested in performing if their concerns were addressed, their responses largely mirrored those of current users. Checking financial account balances or recent transactions was the most commonly cited (32 percent), followed by downloading their bank's mobile banking app (21 percent), transferring money between accounts (20 percent), receiv-

ing alerts from their bank (19 percent), locating the closest in-network ATM or branch (18 percent), depositing checks electronically (17 percent), and making bill payments (15 percent). However, 59 percent of those who do not use mobile banking indicated that they had no interest in performing any mobile banking activities even if their concerns were addressed.

Mobile Payments

For purposes of this survey, mobile payments are defined as "purchases, bill payments, charitable donations, payments to another person, or any other payments made using a mobile phone. You can do this either by accessing a web page through the web browser on your mobile device, by sending a text message (SMS), or by using a downloadable app on your mobile device. The amount of the payment may be applied to your phone bill (for example, Red Cross text message donation), charged to your credit card, deducted from a prepaid card, or withdrawn directly from your bank account."

Adoption Rates

Mobile payments continue to be less common than mobile banking. Based on the responses to the broad definition of mobile payments listed above, 22 percent of those with access to a mobile phone reported that they made a mobile payment in the 12 months prior to the survey, up from 17 percent in 2013, 15 percent in 2012, and 12 percent in 2011. Rates of mobile payment usage are somewhat higher among smartphone users. The share of smartphone users

Table 5. Use of mobile payments in the past 12 months by age Percent, except as noted				
Age group	2011	2012	2013	2014
18–29	20	26	28	34
30–44	16	18	21	31
45–59	8	9	13	16
60+	5	8	7	7
Total	12	15	17	22
Number of respondents	2,002	2,291	2,341	2,603

Note: Percentages are of those in each group who have a mobile phone.

Table 6. Use of mobile payments in the past 12 months by race/ethnicity Percent, except as noted				
Race/ethnicity	2011	2012	2013	2014
White, non-Hispanic	10	13	12	17
Black, non-Hispanic	14	18	34	34
Other, non-Hispanic	15	17	16	24
Hispanic	20	18	26	32
2+ races, non-Hispanic	9	13	31	23
Total	12	15	17	22
Number of respondents	2,002	2,291	2,341	2,603

Note: Percentages are of those in each group who have a mobile phone.

who reported having made a mobile payment in the previous 12 months increased to 28 percent, up from 24 percent in 2013 and 2012, and 23 percent in 2011.

Of current mobile payment users, 16 percent had started using mobile payments in the prior six months, while 13 percent began using mobile payments six to twelve months prior to the survey. A further 21 percent reported that they started using mobile payments in the prior one to two years, and 26 percent reported that they began using mobile payments more than two years prior to the survey. Twenty-two percent of users are unable to recall when they began using mobile payments.

Younger consumers are more likely to make mobile payments (table 5). Of those with a mobile phone in 2014, 34 percent of individuals ages 18 to 29 and 31 percent of individuals ages 30 to 44 had made mobile payments. By comparison, only 7 percent of those ages 60 or over reported making mobile payments. This pattern of use by age has been evident across all four years of the survey.

Among those owning a mobile phone, minorities are more likely to make mobile payments (table 6). In 2014, 34 percent of non-Hispanic blacks with mobile phones and 32 percent of Hispanics with mobile phones had made mobile payments, while only 17 percent of non-Hispanic whites reported making mobile payments. The pattern of minorities making mobile payments at a higher rate than white, non-Hispanic consumers has persisted over time.

There is no clear relationship between mobile payment usage and income or education level among those who own a mobile phone.

Common Mobile Payment Activities

Focusing only on those smartphone owners who reported that they had made a mobile payment in the prior 12 months, the most common mobile payment activity was paying bills (68 percent), followed by making online or in-app purchases (54 percent). The next most common activities reported by mobile payment users were paying for a product or service at a store (39 percent) and transferring money directly to another person in the United States (36 percent). Receiving money from another person using a mobile phone (31 percent) and using an app to receive loyalty or reward points (30 percent) were also relatively common activities for mobile payment users with smartphones. Less common activities were paying for parking, a taxi, or public transit using a mobile phone (16 percent), making a payment by text message (11 percent), and sending a remittance overseas (9 percent). (See box 3 for a research note on measuring the use of mobile payments and mobile banking.)

Although using a mobile phone to pay for a retail purchase at the point-of-sale (POS) is less common than paying bills or making an online or in-app purchase, it is becoming less rare of an occurrence. Developments in technology, the entrance of new market participants, and increased familiarity with mobile payments may be contributing to this trend. As noted above, in 2014, 39 percent of all mobile payments users with smartphones made POS purchases with their mobile phone in the 12 months prior to the survey—a figure in line with the 39 percent who reported such payments in 2013. However, among those POS users, less than half (41 percent) had made a POS payment in the preceding month,

Box 3. Research Note: Measuring the Use of Mobile Payments and Mobile Banking

Over the four years that the Federal Reserve has been conducting this survey, respondents have consistently been asked to gauge whether they had used mobile banking or mobile payments in the preceding 12 months based on general descriptions of these mobile financial services. Responses to those questions provide a baseline for how usage has changed over the course of the survey. However, the number or respondents reporting that they use mobile banking and mobile payments based on the general descriptions is lower than the number reporting that they engage in specific banking or payment activities. This indicates that actual usage may be somewhat higher than the general questions would indicate, and may indicate that more specific questions may prompt respondents to remember details about their usage in a different way. These results also illustrate the challenges for both researchers and respondents in how to categorize mobile banking and payment activities as technologies continue to emerge and evolve and as consumers move from exploration to adoption of new ways of using their smartphones.

For example, mobile payment users were identified by a general question about whether they have engaged in any mobile payments activities over the past 12 months.[1] In addition, mobile phone users were asked whether they had used their phone for particular mobile payments tasks. Some respondents who answered "no" to the mobile payments question indicated they have done one or more of these mobile payments tasks, implying the share of people making mobile payments may be higher than the measure of mobile payments users based on the general definition. In the 2014 survey, 28 percent of smartphone owners were identified as

mobile payments users based on their response to the general question. By comparison, 47 percent of smartphone owners reported completing at least one mobile payments task, regardless of their answer to the general question about mobile payments.[2]

Figure A shows the share of respondents with a smartphone who reported completing mobile payments tasks, grouped by whether they indicated they used mobile payments. The lighter bars represent respondents who said they had used a particular form of mobile payment but had answered "no" to the more general question about whether they had used any form of mobile payment.

A similar pattern is evident with the questions on mobile banking. Thirty-nine percent of those with mobile phones and bank accounts reported using mobile banking in the prior 12 months based on the general question. By comparison, 50 percent of respondents with mobile phones and bank accounts reported completing one or more specific mobile banking tasks, regardless of their answer to the general question about mobile banking.

These results illustrate that technology adoption can be viewed as a continuum, both in terms of the types and frequency of activities involved and in terms of how respondents view and report their activities. The majority of respondents were consistent in providing responses indicating they were either users or non-users of these services in their answers to both the general questions and the

(continued on next page)

---

[1] For the explanation of mobile payments provided to respondents, see page 14.

[2] For all those with mobile phones, including both feature phones and smartphones, 22 percent reported making mobile payments based on the general definition and 36 percent reported completing at least one mobile payments task, regardless of their answer to the general question about mobile payments.

---

and less than a quarter had made more than two such payments.

Scanning a QR code displayed on a mobile phone is the most common method that consumers use to make mobile payments at the point of sale, used by 31 percent of those mobile payment users with smartphones who had made mobile POS payments.[14] While this remains the most common POS mobile

payment, it is a decrease from 39 percent a year ago. The next most common POS methods were making a payment using a mobile app that does not require scanning a barcode or tapping their device (22 percent), and making a payment by waving or tapping

---

[14] A Quick Response (QR) code is a type of barcode that quickly transfers information to a device when scanned. Some mobile payment applications use QR codes displayed on the user's smartphone screen to communicate the payment credentials to merchants when scanned at the POS.

Respondents who answered that, using their mobile phone, they had "Paid for a product or service at a store (including at gas pumps and for restaurant meals)" were asked a follow up question (question 39) asking about ways of paying in a store. The follow up question listed four ways of paying with a phone, including "Other (Please Specify)." However, 58 percent of those who were asked this follow up question refused the question or did not select any of these four options.

Box 3. Research Note: Measuring the Use of Mobile Payments and Mobile Banking–*continued*

Figure A. Mobile payment tasks for smartphone users, by mobile payment self-identification

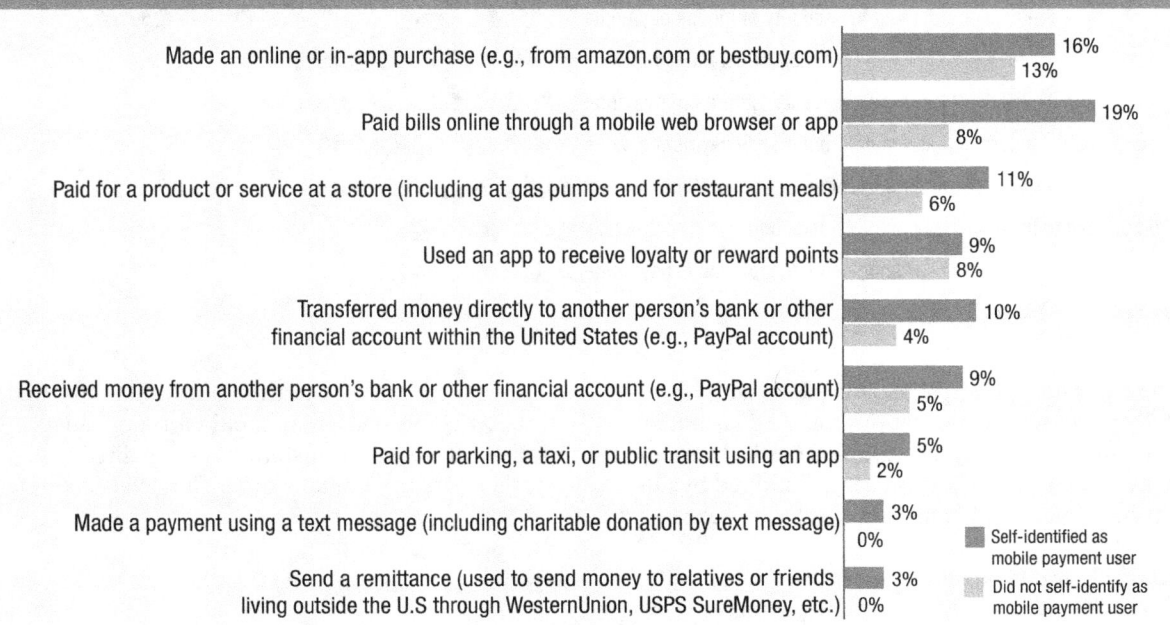

specific task questions, although there was less consistency in the responses for mobile payments use than for mobile banking use.[3] Those respondents

who provided seemingly anomalous answers did report less frequent use of the specific services cited than respondents who said "yes" to the general question as well as the more specific ones. For this reason, it is possible that some consumers are "dabblers" in mobile services but do not consider themselves more general users of the technology. It is also possible that different questions simply prompted different responses or that some respondents misremembered and answered incorrectly.

[3] Overall, 73 percent of smartphone owners provided consistent responses on the mobile payments questions: 25 percent self-identified as mobile payments users in response to the general question and also reported at least one mobile payments task, while 49 percent self-identified as not using mobile payments based on the general question and reported no mobile payments tasks. Overall, 86 percent of those with mobile phones and bank accounts provided consistent responses to the mobile banking questions: 38 percent self-identified as mobile banking users in response to the general question and reported at least one mobile banking task, while 48 percent self-identified as not using

mobile banking based on the general question and reported no mobile banking tasks.

their mobile phone at the POS terminal (14 percent).[15]

[15] The most commonly reported mobile payments services used in the last year were PayPal (43 percent), Starbucks (11 percent), Google Wallet (9 percent), and Apple Pay (5 percent). Forty-three percent of those who were asked the question about mobile payment services (question 42) refused to provide an answer. This question was asked of all those with smartphones who had made a mobile payment in the last year. Because the answer choices did not include options such as "Other" or "Do

Mobile payments are most commonly funded using debit cards (55 percent), credit cards (51 percent), directly from a bank account (41 percent), or from an account at a non-financial institution such as PayPal (15 percent). Only 8 percent of mobile payment users reported that they used a prepaid debit card, and 4 percent had the charge directly applied to their

not know," refusing to answer would have been a likely response for those who have not used these services.

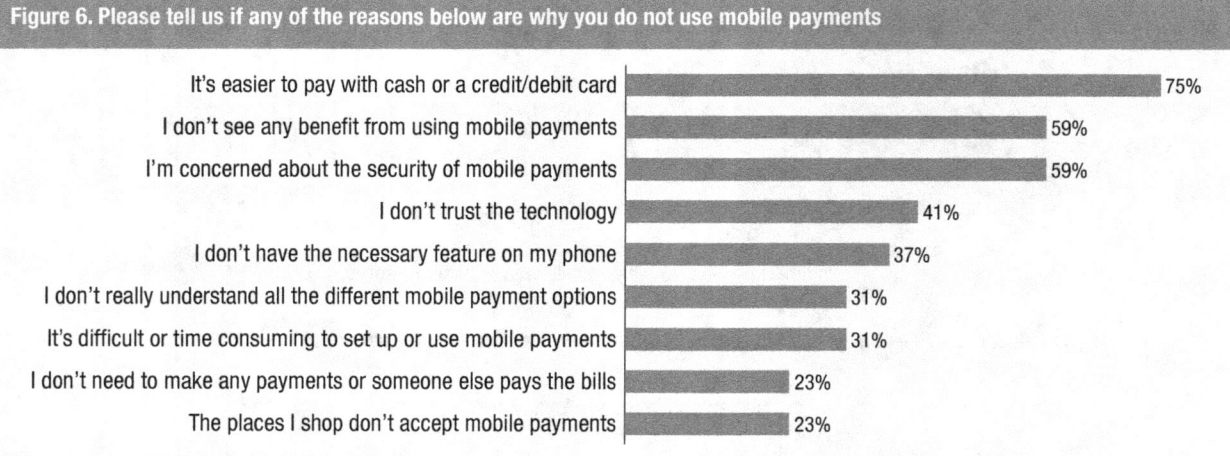

Figure 6. Please tell us if any of the reasons below are why you do not use mobile payments

It's easier to pay with cash or a credit/debit card	75%
I don't see any benefit from using mobile payments	59%
I'm concerned about the security of mobile payments	59%
I don't trust the technology	41%
I don't have the necessary feature on my phone	37%
I don't really understand all the different mobile payment options	31%
It's difficult or time consuming to set up or use mobile payments	31%
I don't need to make any payments or someone else pays the bills	23%
The places I shop don't accept mobile payments	23%

Note: The number of respondents was 2,137.

phone bill. The type of payment used to fund the mobile purchase has implications for the consumer protections that the payer is afforded on the transaction, as different payment sources are covered by different consumer regulations and regulatory agencies.[16]

Among all mobile payments users, the median reported frequency of using mobile payments was two times in the month prior to the survey. As with mobile banking, there is variation among mobile payments users in how frequently they use the service and in types of activities. Twenty-seven percent of mobile payments users reported they had used mobile payments in the past 12 months but not in the month prior to the survey. Like the overall group of mobile payments users, the most common mobile payment activity reported by these low-intensity users was paying bills (31 percent).

Eighteen percent of mobile payments users reported that they had used mobile payments more than five times in the month prior to the survey. Compared to all mobile payment users, these high-intensity mobile payment users had higher rates of engaging in all mobile payments activities and tended to engage in a few mobile payment activities at much higher rates.[17] High-intensity users more frequently made an online

or in-app purchase, paid their bills online through a mobile web browser or app, paid for a product or service at a store, and transferred money directly to another person's bank or other financial account.

Reasons for Using—or Not Using—Mobile Payments

Getting a smartphone is the most common reason given by consumers who have newly adopted mobile payment activity (34 percent). Convenience is the second-most common reason people started using mobile payments (29 percent). The ability to make mobile payments becoming available to them was cited by 16 percent of users, while 9 percent indicated that they began using mobile payments because they became comfortable with the security.

Among those who do not use mobile payments, the main reason they have not adopted the technology is that they prefer to use other means of making payments: 75 percent reported that it is easier to pay with other methods. Fifty-nine percent did not see a benefit from using mobile payments; the same proportion cited security concerns (figure 6). The incidence of reasons for not using mobile payments was generally consistent between the 2013 and 2014 surveys. However, in the 2014 survey, concerns about the security of mobile payments decreased from 63 percent in 2013. Also, fewer respondents reported that not having the necessary features on their phone (46 percent in 2013), not understanding mobile payment options (37 percent in 2013), and the places they shopped not accepting mobile payments (27 per-

---

[16] For further details on how existing consumer regulations relate to the various methods for making mobile payments, see Stephanie Martin (2012), "Statement before the Committee on Financial Services Subcommittee on Financial Institutions and Consumer Credit U.S. House of Representatives" (Washington: Federal Reserve Board, June), www.federalreserve.gov/newsevents/testimony/martin20120629a.pdf.

[17] For the purposes of this report, "high-intensity" mobile payments users are identified as those respondents who have used mobile payments within the year prior to the 2014 survey and have used mobile payments more frequently than 75 percent of

all mobile payments users, which corresponds to a frequency greater than five times in the month prior to the 2014 survey.

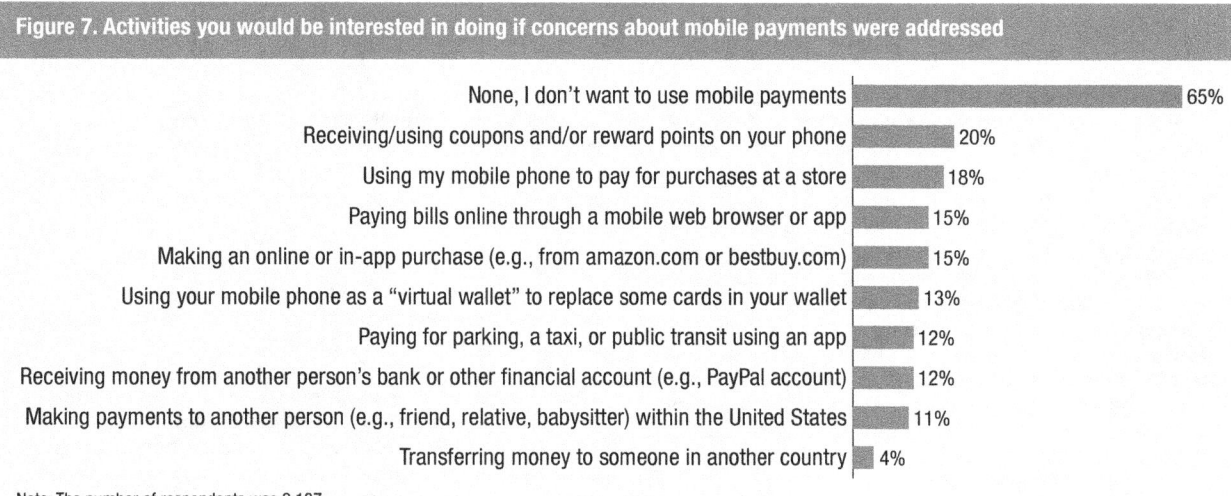

Figure 7. Activities you would be interested in doing if concerns about mobile payments were addressed

Activity	Percent
None, I don't want to use mobile payments	65%
Receiving/using coupons and/or reward points on your phone	20%
Using my mobile phone to pay for purchases at a store	18%
Paying bills online through a mobile web browser or app	15%
Making an online or in-app purchase (e.g., from amazon.com or bestbuy.com)	15%
Using your mobile phone as a "virtual wallet" to replace some cards in your wallet	13%
Paying for parking, a taxi, or public transit using an app	12%
Receiving money from another person's bank or other financial account (e.g., PayPal account)	12%
Making payments to another person (e.g., friend, relative, babysitter) within the United States	11%
Transferring money to someone in another country	4%

Note: The number of respondents was 2,137.

cent in 2013) were reasons why they had not used mobile payments.

For those worried about the security of mobile payments, the concerns roughly mirror those about mobile banking. The main fears associated with mobile payments include the interception of payment information (21 percent), phone "hacking" (13 percent), lost or stolen phones (10 percent), misuse of personal information (3 percent), and malware or viruses installed on their phone (2 percent). As with mobile banking, the most common response was that respondents were concerned with all of those security risks (51 percent).

When consumers who do not use mobile payments were asked to indicate all the mobile payment activities they would have an interest in using if their concerns were addressed, 65 percent indicated that they simply had no interest in using mobile payments even if their concerns were addressed. This is similar to the responses regarding mobile banking, indicating that some consumers simply have no interest in utilizing the new technology under any circumstances. Of the potential activities of interest to others, receiving/using coupons on their phone was the most commonly cited (20 percent), followed by using a mobile phone to pay for purchases at a store (18 percent) (figure 7).

When those with a smartphone who did not report making POS payments were asked if they plan to use their mobile phone to make a payment in a store in the next 12 months, 5 percent said they "definitely will" and 16 percent said they "probably will." The majority of smartphone users said that they "prob-ably will not" (44 percent) or "definitely will not" (35 percent) use their phone to make an in-store payment.

Mobile Security

One of the main reservations consumers have with adopting mobile banking and mobile payments is concern about the security of the technology. Despite the increased prevalence of mobile banking and mobile payments, a significant share of consumers believe the technology to be unsafe or do not know how safe it is (see box 4 for a discussion of industry developments in securing mobile payments). Among all mobile phone users, 25 percent believed that people's personal information is "somewhat unsafe" when using mobile banking and 19 percent believed that it is "very unsafe." A further 15 percent of mobile phone users simply did not know how safe it is to use mobile banking. Only 7 percent said it is "very safe" to use mobile banking (table 7).

When mobile phone users were asked how safe they believe people's personal financial information is when they use a mobile phone to pay for a purchase at a store, 28 percent said it was "somewhat unsafe" and 21 percent said it was "very unsafe." As with mobile banking, there exists significant uncertainty about the security of POS mobile payments, with 15 percent saying they "don't know" whether people's personal financial information is safe when making such a payment. The share of consumers who said that POS mobile payments were "very safe" was only 5 percent, while 30 percent said that it was "somewhat safe" (table 8).

Box 4. Industry Developments in Securing Mobile Payments

Interest and adoption of mobile payment services may be poised for growth as a number of developments in technology and security take hold in the mobile financial marketplace. In this and preceding surveys, concerns about the security of mobile payment technologies are frequently cited by non-users as reasons for not using mobile payments. Consumers have also cited, to a lesser extent, the lack of necessary features on their phone and the lack of acceptance of mobile payments at places where they shop as reasons for not using mobile payments.[1] Recent efforts to enhance the security of mobile payment transactions and to apply emerging technologies to a payments context could shape consumers' attitudes about and use of mobile payments in the coming years.

This survey's results confirm that security concerns are on the minds of many consumers. The payments industry is taking steps to enhance transaction security at various points in the process, including by working toward conversion to EMV (named after its founders Europay, MasterCard, and Visa), a standard payment specification for authorizing credit and debit chip-card transactions. (This technology is also referred to as "chip and pin" or "chip and signature.") In order to accept in-person EMV transactions, merchants install EMV-compliant checkout terminals in their stores, and card issuers provide consumers with new cards containing microchips that meet the EMV standard. To encourage merchants and card issuers to adopt this technology, the card networks have set a deadline of October 2015, after

which they intend to shift liability for fraudulent transactions to the party that is not EMV-compliant. While not a mobile-specific development, EMV conversion ought to decrease the forms of certain types of payment fraud, and could influence consumer preferences over time.

Increasingly, smartphone manufacturers are also equipping devices with hardware and software to provide more payment options—such as Near Field Communications (NFC) antennas to interact with in-store check-out NFC-enabled terminals—and security features—such as fingerprint authentication technology. Many new EMV terminals are likely to also support NFC technology. Security-minded consumers may have more confidence making a mobile payment from a device that uses multiple layers of security, complies with EMV standards, and/or offers new or additional features. While these efforts are largely undertaken by the private sector, an October 2014 Executive Order establishing EMV as the standard for federal government payments may reinforce private actions.[2]

The changes in the marketplace may ultimately better protect customers' data by reducing the amount of data accessed and stored by merchants. New payment card technology that replaces the real card number with a substitute value (also known as a token) may also make it more difficult to use card information—on mobile devices or in other forms—fraudulently. If successful, these efforts could improve consumer confidence in newer payments technology in general, possibly affecting the related use of mobile payments.

---

[1] In the 2014 survey, 37 percent of non-mobile payments users cited the lack of necessary features on their phone and 23 percent cited the lack of acceptance of mobile payments at places where they shop as reasons for not using mobile payments.

[2] See www.whitehouse.gov/the-press-office/2014/10/17/fact-sheet-safeguarding-consumers-financial-security.

In addition, there is a dichotomy in perceived security among users and non-users of mobile banking services. Among mobile phone owners who do not

use mobile banking, only 3 percent rated the overall security of mobile banking as "very safe," while 24 percent rated it "somewhat safe." Nineteen per-

Table 7. How safe do you believe people's personal information is when they use mobile banking? Percent, except as noted		
	2013	2014
Very safe	6	7
Somewhat safe	32	34
Somewhat unsafe	25	25
Very unsafe	18	19
Don't know	17	15
Number of respondents	2,341	2,603

Table 8. How safe do you believe people's personal information is when they use a mobile phone to pay for a purchase at a store? Percent, except as noted		
	2013	2014
Very safe	4	5
Somewhat safe	30	30
Somewhat unsafe	27	28
Very unsafe	19	21
Don't know	18	15
Number of respondents	2,341	2,603

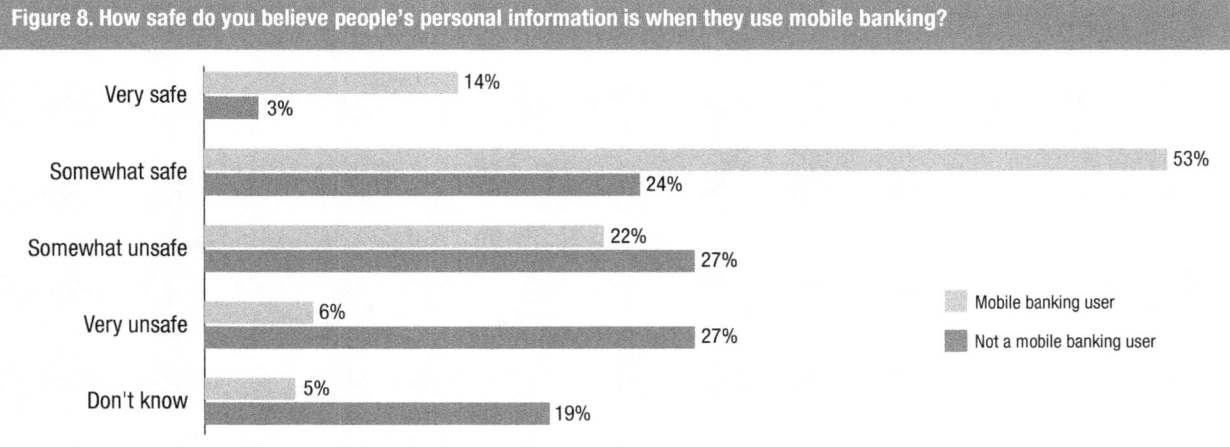

Figure 8. How safe do you believe people's personal information is when they use mobile banking?

Note: The number of respondents was 829 mobile banking users and 1,584 non-users of mobile banking.

cent of non-users indicated that they "don't know" how safe it is to use mobile banking. Mobile banking users, however, rated mobile banking as "very safe" (14 percent) or "somewhat safe" (53 percent) in maintaining their personal information. Only 5 percent of mobile banking users indicated that they "don't know" how safe mobile banking is at protecting their personal information (figure 8).

Interest in Mobile Services

Mobile phone users expressed significant interest in expanding the range of functions they could perform with their phones. Consumers were asked to select the types of activity they would be interested in performing with their mobile phones, assuming the function were made available to them (figure 9). Some consumers appear to be open to greater use of their phones as a tool to get the best prices in their shopping activities: 24 percent expressed an interest in using their mobile phones to compare prices while shopping; 26 percent indicate that they would like to receive and manage discount offers and coupons; and 24 percent would like to receive location-based offers. They also expressed an interest in using their phones to store gift cards or track loyalty/reward points (19 percent) and to manage their personal finances (13 percent).

Although consumers might be willing to use their phones to improve shopping experiences, many are resistant to sharing their current location and personal information with companies they shop with regularly (figure 10). Smartphone users were asked about their level of agreement with the statement "I am willing to allow my mobile phone to provide my location to companies I shop with regularly so that they can offer me discounts, promotions, or services based on where I am." There appears to be significant discomfort with providing one's location to companies, as 33 percent indicated that they "disagree" and 26 percent "strongly disagree."

Consumers reported being even less willing to allow their phones to be used to provide companies with their personal information in order to receive targeted discounts, promotions, and offers. When smartphone owners were asked about their level of agreement with the statement "I am willing to allow my mobile phone to provide personal information such as my sex, age, friends, and shopping history to companies I shop with regularly so that they can offer me targeted discounts, promotions, or services," 37 percent chose "disagree" and 39 percent chose "strongly disagree."

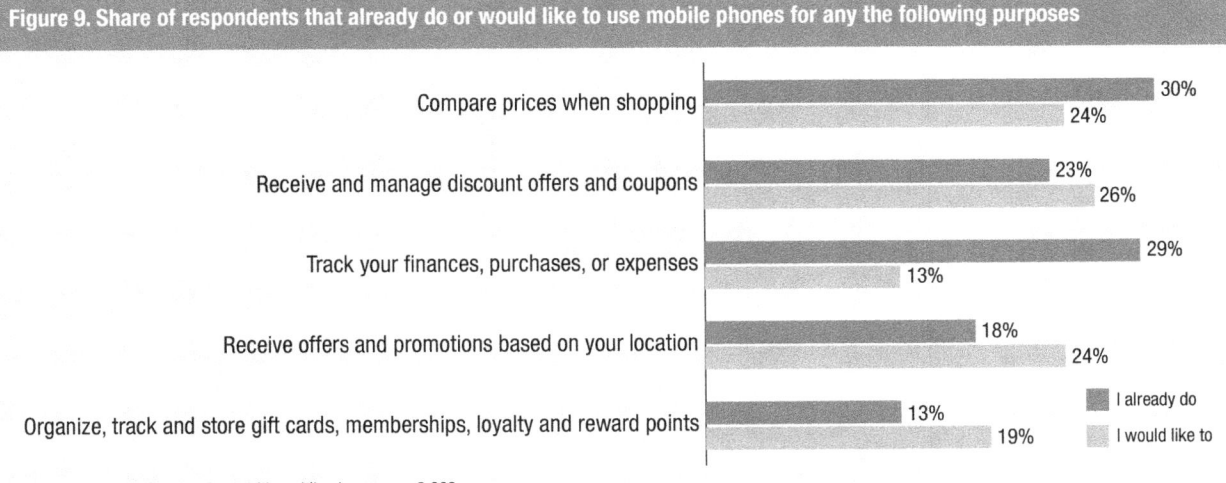

Figure 9. Share of respondents that already do or would like to use mobile phones for any the following purposes

Compare prices when shopping — 30% (I already do), 24% (I would like to)

Receive and manage discount offers and coupons — 23% (I already do), 26% (I would like to)

Track your finances, purchases, or expenses — 29% (I already do), 13% (I would like to)

Receive offers and promotions based on your location — 18% (I already do), 24% (I would like to)

Organize, track and store gift cards, memberships, loyalty and reward points — 13% (I already do), 19% (I would like to)

Note: The number of respondents with mobile phones was 2,603.

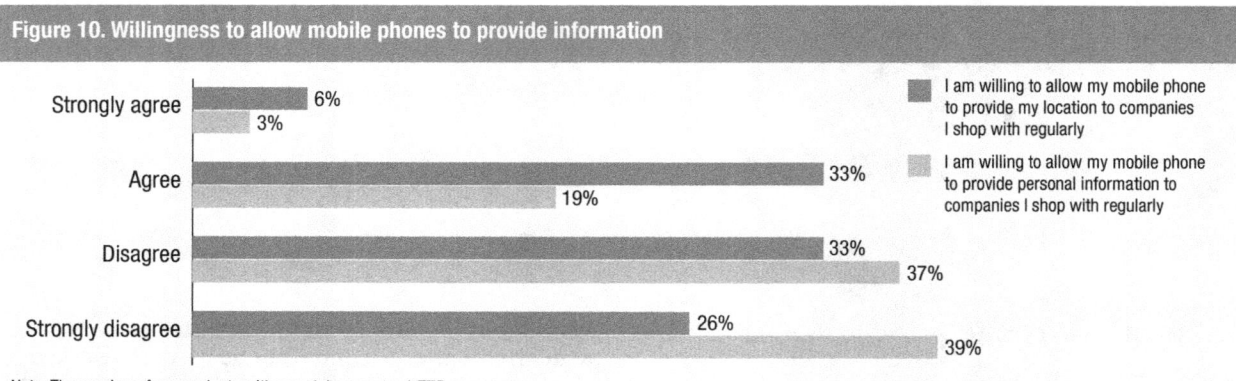

Figure 10. Willingness to allow mobile phones to provide information

Strongly agree — 6% / 3%
Agree — 33% / 19%
Disagree — 33% / 37%
Strongly disagree — 26% / 39%

- I am willing to allow my mobile phone to provide my location to companies I shop with regularly
- I am willing to allow my mobile phone to provide personal information to companies I shop with regularly

Note: The number of respondents with smartphones was 1,775.

In-Store Product Research and Price Comparison

Consumers are using their mobile phones to comparison shop and obtain product information while in retail stores. The prevalence of smartphones with barcode scanning software and Internet access has altered consumer behavior in the retail environment. With this technology, consumers can compare prices across retailers while in a store or online, or locate an item that is out of stock. Retailers have coined the term "showrooming" to describe the practice of consumers going to retail stores to examine products and then purchasing them online.

Among smartphone owners, 47 percent said that they have used their mobile phone to comparison shop on the Internet while at a retail store, and 33 percent have used a barcode scanning application for price comparisons. Consumers are also using their smartphones to obtain product information: 31 percent have scanned a QR code in a newspaper, magazine, or billboard advertisement to obtain information about a product, and 42 percent have used their phone to get product reviews or product information while shopping at a retail store.

Many consumers who use their smartphone to comparison shop reported that they altered their decisions as a result: 69 percent who have comparison shopped in a store reported that they changed where they made a purchase after comparing prices, and 79 percent reported that they changed what they purchased as a result of reading product reviews on their smartphone while at a retail store.

As the use of mobile banking increases, mobile phones are increasingly becoming tools for managing personal finances and controlling spending. For example, 63 percent of mobile banking users with smartphones report using their mobile phone to check account balances or available credit before making a large purchase in the 12 months prior to the survey. Of those who checked their balance or available credit, 53 percent reported that they decided not to buy an item because of the amount of money in their bank account or the amount of available credit. Many consumers have near-constant access to their mobile phones, and these results illustrate that

these devices have the potential to provide "just-in-time information" that can influence consumer financial behavior.

In addition, mobile phones can provide readily accessible and timely prompts that may help consumers make different, and perhaps smarter, financial decisions. The actions consumers take in response to the receipt of text message or e-mail notices from their financial institutions demonstrate some of the potential effects of this technology for encouraging consumers to engage in different financial behaviors that may prove to have beneficial outcomes.

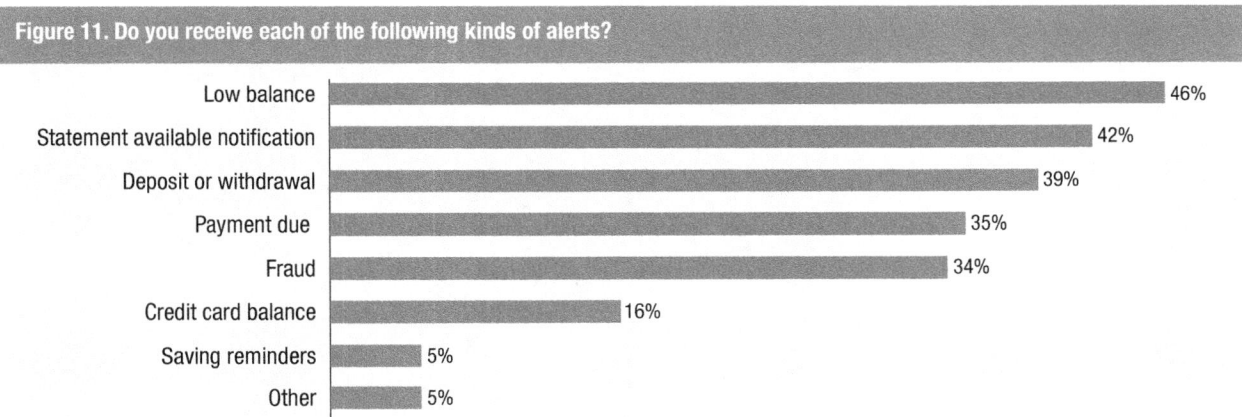

Figure 11. Do you receive each of the following kinds of alerts?

Note: The number of respondents who were mobile banking users was 459. Respondents may receive alerts from their financial institution via push notification, text message, or e-mail.

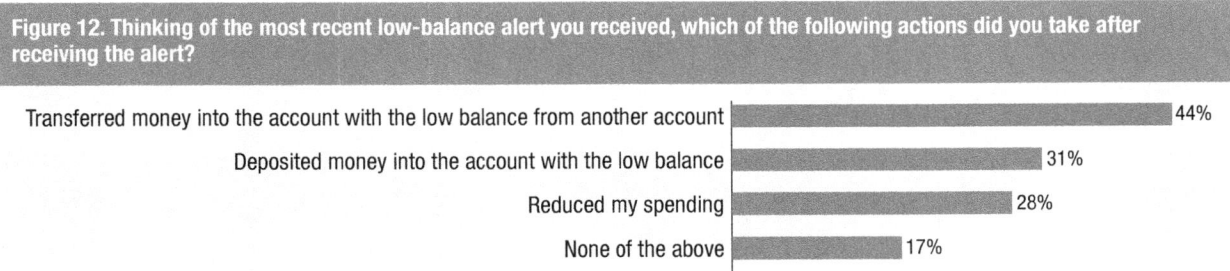

Figure 12. Thinking of the most recent low-balance alert you received, which of the following actions did you take after receiving the alert?

Note: The number of respondents who were mobile banking users was 211.

More than half (57 percent) of people who use mobile banking receive alerts from their bank (figure 11). Nearly all mobile banking users who received a low-balance alert from their bank reported taking some action in response: transferring money into the account with the low-balance (44 percent), reducing their spending (28 percent), or depositing additional money into the account (31 percent) (figure 12). Only 17 percent reported taking no action in response to receiving a low-balance alert.

As smartphones become more common and more versatile, they can play an increasingly large role in the interactions between consumers and financial service providers, retailers, and other businesses. The near-constant presence of mobile phones in consumers' lives also makes them a potentially useful tool for the delivery of just-in-time financial information or as an aid in decisionmaking. Given the prevalence of mobile phones—particularly smartphones—among minorities, low-income individuals, and younger persons, mobile technology has the potential to empower consumers and expand access to financial services for underserved populations. However, consumers will need to understand and weigh the perceived benefits and potential risks to their security and privacy presented by the use of this evolving technology.

The use of mobile banking has increased substantially in the past year and appears likely to continue to increase as more consumers use smartphones or recognize the convenience of this service, and as more financial institutions offer mobile banking. The most common tasks for mobile banking users continue to be checking account balances and transferring funds. Use of the remote deposit capture feature continues to grow steadily. The use of mobile payments, broadly defined, also increased from 2013 to 2014. Paying bills online and making online or in-app purchases are the most common mobile payment activities, followed by making a POS payment. Among mobile payments users with smartphones, the use of mobile phones to make payments at the POS is essentially unchanged from the 2013 survey.

The main factors limiting consumer adoption of mobile banking and payments are a preference for using other methods for banking or making payments and security concerns. In terms of the value proposition to consumers, the significant number of mobile users who reported an interest in using their phones to receive discounts, coupons, and promotions or to track rewards and loyalty points suggests that tying these services to a mobile payment service may increase the attractiveness of mobile phones as a means of payment.

In order to create a nationally representative probability-based sample, GfK's KnowledgePanel® has selected respondents based on both random digit dialing and address-based sampling (ABS). Since 2009, new respondents have been recruited using ABS. To recruit respondents, GfK sends out mailings to a random selection of residential postal addresses. Out of 100 mailings, approximately 14 households respond to GfK and express an interest in joining the panel. Of those who express an interest in joining, around 64 percent complete the process and become members of the panel.[18] If the person contacted is interested in participating but does not have a computer or Internet access, GfK provides him or her with a laptop and Internet. Panel respondents are continuously lost to attrition and added to replenish the panel, so the recruitment rate and enrollment rate may vary over time.

For the 2014 mobile survey, a total of 6,892 KnowledgePanel® members received e-mail invitations to complete the survey, including both the primary sample and a rural oversample. The primary sample included a random selection of 2,308 out of the 2,657 KnowledgePanel® respondents who participated in the Board's 2013 mobile survey and an additional 2,657 randomly selected KnowledgePanel® respondents who did not participate in the Board's previous survey. (See table 1 in main text.) From these two components of the primary sample, a total of 2,925 people (excluding breakoffs) responded to the e-mail request to participate and completed the survey, yielding a final stage completion rate of 58.9 percent. The recruitment rate for the primary sample, reported by GfK, was 14.6 percent and the profile rate was 64.0 percent, for a cumulative response rate of 5.5 percent. Answers from these respondents were used to compute statistics presented in the main body of the report, as well as in the tables in appendix 3.

The 2014 survey also included an oversample of respondents residing in rural areas as defined by Rural Urban Commuting Area (RUCA) codes.[19] Respondents were selected for inclusion in the rural oversample if the ZIP code for their residence was classified as being in RUCA codes 7.0-10.3. Because RUCA codes are assigned at the Census tract level, ZIP codes meeting this criteria were identified based on the crosswalk available from the Center for Rural Health at the University of North Dakota. (See ruralhealth.und.edu/ruca.) All members of KnowledgePanel® residing in rural areas based on this definition, but not already included in one of the other two samples, received an invitation to respond to the survey. Of these additional 1,927 KnowledgePanel® members who received invitations as a part of the rural oversample, 1,298 people (excluding breakoffs) responded to the e-mail request to participate and completed the survey, yielding a final stage completion rate of 67.4 percent for the oversample. The recruitment rate for the rural oversample, reported by GfK, was 14.4 percent and the profile rate was 63.3 percent, for a cumulative response rate of 6.1 percent. Answers from these respondents were combined with answers from the other two samples and used to compute statistics presented in box 1 of the report.

To enhance the completion rate, GfK sent e-mail reminders to non-responders on days three and ten of the field period. GfK maintains an ongoing modest incentive program to encourage KnowledgePanel® members to participate. Incentives take the form of raffles and lotteries with cash and other prizes. KnowlegePanel® members who were a part of the rural oversample in the 2014 survey were offered an additional $5 incentive for completion of the survey.

Significant resources and infrastructure are devoted to the recruitment process for the KnowledgePanel®

---

[18] For further details on the KnowledgePanel® sampling methodology and comparisons between KnowledgePanel® and telephone surveys see www.knowledgenetworks.com/accuracy/spring2010/disogra-spring10.html.

[19] Information on RUCA codes is available from the U.S. Department of Agriculture's Economic Research Service. (See www.ers.usda.gov/data-products/rural-urban-commuting-area-codes.aspx.)

so that the resulting panel can properly represent the adult population of the United States. Consequently, the raw distribution of KnowledgePanel® mirrors that of the U.S. adults fairly closely, baring occasional disparities that may emerge for certain subgroups due to differential attrition rates among recruited panel members.

The selection methodology for general population samples from the KnowledgePanel® ensures that the resulting samples behave as an equal probability of selection method (EPSEM) samples. This methodology starts by weighting the entire KnowledgePanel® to the benchmarks secured from the latest March supplement of the Current Population Survey (CPS) along several dimensions. This way, the weighted distribution of the KnowledgePanel® matches that of the U.S. adults. Typically, the geo-demographic dimensions used for weighting the entire KnowledgePanel® include gender, age, race/ethnicity, education, Census region, household income, home ownership status, metropolitan area status, and Internet access.

Using the above weights as the measure of size (MOS) for each panel member, in the next step a probability proportional to size (PPS) procedure is used to select study specific samples. Since this survey includes a rural oversample, the departure caused by this oversample from an EPSEM design are corrected by adjusting the corresponding design weights accordingly with the CPS benchmarks serving as reference points.

Once the sample has been selected and fielded, and all the study data are collected and made final, a post-stratification process is used to adjust for any survey non-response as well as any non-coverage or under- and over-sampling resulting from the study-specific sample design. The following variables were used for the adjustment of weights for this study: gender, age, race/ethnicity, education, Census region, residence in a metropolitan area, access to the Internet, and residence in a rural area according to the definition used for the rural oversample. Demographic and geographic distributions for the non-institutionalized, civilian population ages 18 and over from the March 2014 CPS are used as benchmarks in this adjustment. For the geographic distribution of residence in a rural setting, the full set of members of KnowledgePanel® was used to generate the benchmark since the CPS does not provide statistics on rural status according to the criteria used to select the oversample.

Although weights allow the sample population to match the U.S. population based on observable characteristics, similar to all survey methods, it remains possible that non-coverage or non-response results in differences between the sample population and the U.S. population that are not corrected using weights.

There are several reasons that a probability-based Internet panel was selected as the method for this survey rather than an alternative survey method. The first reason is that these types of Internet surveys have been found to be representative of the population.[20] The second reason is that the ABS Internet panel allows the same respondents to be re-interviewed in subsequent surveys with relative ease, as they remain in the panel for several years. The third reason is that Internet panel surveys have numerous existing data points on respondents from previously administered surveys, including detailed demographic and economic information. This allows for the inclusion of additional information on respondents without increasing respondent burden. Lastly, collecting data through an ABS Internet panel survey is cost effective, and can be done relatively quickly.

There are possible questions about the extent to which results from an online survey of technology use can be interpreted as being representative of the technology use of the U.S. population. As with any survey method, Internet panels can be subject to biases resulting from undercoverage or nonresponse and, in this case, potential underrepresentation of adults who are physically or cognitively impaired or who may prefer not to use some forms of technology. Not everyone in the United States has access to the Internet and there are demographic (income, education, age) and geographic (urban and rural) differences between those who do have access and those who do not. These concerns are partially corrected by GfK providing Internet access to respondents who do not have it in order to include the portion of the population that does not have Internet access in KnowledgePanel®. They are further corrected by the use of post-stratification weights to ensure that the Internet usage and key demographics of the weighted sample population matches the entire U.S. population. That said, participation in this type of survey

---

[20] David S. Yeager, Jon A. Krosnick, LinChiat Chang, Harold S. Javitz, Matthew S. Levendusky, Alberto Simpser, and Rui Wang (2011), "Comparing the Accuracy of RDD Telephone Surveys and Internet Surveys Conducted with Probability and Non-Probability Samples," *Public Opinion Quarterly, vol. 75(4),* pp. 709–47.

may require a certain level of skill and interest in responding online, which could limit coverage of some groups, particularly among those in the population who are less likely to use computers or the Internet. As a result, to the extent that these differences cannot be incorporated into the sample weights, technology usage among survey respondents may differ along key dimensions from that of the overall U.S. population.

Below is a reproduction of the survey instrument in its entirety. The bracketed text are programming instructions that (1) indicate whether or not a question is single choice [SP] or multiple choice [MP] and (2) represent any skip pattern used to reach that question and which questions should be grouped together on a page. The respondents only saw the questions and response options; they did not see the program code.

[DISPLAY]

OMB Control Number: 7100-0359

Expiration Date: 04/30/2017

For more information, click here.

The Federal Reserve Board is interested in learning more about how people manage their finances, shop, and make payments. We are also interested in how people interact with financial institutions, and how mobile phones and other technology facilitate these interactions. The information collected in this survey will be used for research, analysis, and policymaking. A dataset containing anonymized responses may also be released publicly on the Federal Reserve Board's website. We appreciate your participation in this survey.

To begin, we are going to ask a few questions about the types of financial products and services that you use.

[PROGRAM INSTRUCTION]

[If "For more information…" clicked, display this text in a new tab or window]

The Federal Reserve may not conduct or sponsor, and an organization is not required to respond to, a collection of information unless it displays a currently valid OMB control number. Public reporting burden for this information collection is estimated to average 0.18 hours, including the time to gather data in the required form and to review instructions and complete the information collection. Send comments regarding this burden estimate or any other aspect of this collection of information, including suggestions for reducing this burden to: Secretary, Board of Governors of the Federal Reserve System, 20th and C Streets, NW, Washington, DC 20551, and to the Office of Management and Budget, Paperwork Reduction Project (7100-0359), Washington, DC 20503.

Banking Section

[SP][SAME AS Q1 IN S16674]

1. Do you or does your spouse/partner currently have some type of bank or credit union account such as a checking, savings, or money market account?

   a. Yes

   b. No

[SP, IF Q1 = B][SAME AS Q2 IN S16674]

2. Have you or your spouse/partner ever had some type of bank or credit union account such as a checking, savings, or money market account?

   a. Yes

   b. No

[SP]

4a. A prepaid debit card, also known as a general purpose prepaid card, is loaded with money and can be used to make payments in stores and online. It works much like a debit card except that it is not connected to a traditional bank account. A prepaid debit card is NOT a credit card.

Have you used a prepaid debit card in the past 12 months?

   a. Yes

   b. No

[SP]

5. Remittances are used to send money to relatives or friends living outside the U.S. For example money can be sent through a bank, WesternUnion, or an app on your mobile phone.

Have you sent a remittance in the past 12 months?

   a. Yes

   b. No

[SP]

5a. In the past 12 months, have you used a money order, check cashing service, pawn shop loan, auto title loan, paycheck advance/deposit advance, or a pay-day loan?

   a. Yes

   b. No

[IF Q1 = A; DISPLAY; SHOW ON THE SAME SCREEN AS Q16]

In this section we would like to ask you about how you interact with your bank or credit union.

[IF Q1 = A; NUMBER BOXES; RANGE: 1-3; UNIQUE VALUES; SHOW ON SAME SCREEN AS DISPLAY]

16. What are the three main ways you (or your spouse/partner) interact with your bank or credit union when you use your accounts? Use number 1 for most often, 2 for 2nd most often, 3 for 3rd most often used. (You can stop numbering below if all the ways you interact with your bank or credit union are covered in less than three responses).

    a. ATM/Cash machine

    b. A teller in person at a branch

    c. Mail

    d. Phone – Talking or using touchtone service

    e. Over the Internet using a computer/tablet

    f. Mobile phone app, mobile web browser, or SMS/text message

    g. Family member, friend, or neighbor does the banking for me

    h. Other (please specify):**[TXT]**_____

[SP, IF Q1 = A]

6. Have you visited a bank branch and spoken with **a teller or a bank employee** in the past 12 months?

   a. Yes

   b. No

[IF Q6=A; NUMBER BOX; RANGE: 0-99]

7. In the past **month,** about how many times have you visited a branch and spoken with a teller or a bank employee? If none enter "0". _____times in the past month

[SP, IF Q1=A]

8. Which of the following best describes the location of your bank or credit union branch that you typically visit when you need to speak with a teller or bank employee?

   a. I visit a branch close to my home, work, school or other place I go to frequently.

   b. I must go out of my way or travel for a while to visit a branch.

   c. I am not able to visit a branch because my bank does not have a branch in my area.

   d. I do not need to visit a branch.

[IF Q8= A OR B; NUMBER BOX; RANGE: 0-999]

9. About how long does it take you to travel to the branch you typically visit (one way)? _____ minutes

[SP, IF Q1 = A]

10. Have you used an **ATM** for any banking transactions in the past 12 months?

    a. Yes

    b. No

[IF Q10=A; NUMBER BOX; RANGE: 0-99]

11. In the past **month**, about how many times have you used an **ATM** for banking transactions? If none enter "0". _____times in the past month

[SP, IF Q1=A]

12. Which of the following best describes the location of the ATM that you typically use for banking transactions?

    a. I use an ATM close to my home, work, school or other place I go to frequently.

    b. I must go out of my way or travel for a while to access the ATM.

    c. I am not able to use an ATM for banking transactions because there is not an ATM in my area.

    d. I do not use an ATM.

[IF Q12=A OR B; NUMBER BOX; RANGE: 0-999]

13. About how long does it take you to travel to the ATM you typically visit (one way)? _____ minutes

[SP, IF Q1 = A]

14. **Telephone banking** is when you access your account by calling a phone number that your bank has provided. You interact with the system using either voice commands, your phone's numeric keypad, or speaking with a live customer service representative. It does not include accessing your bank using the internet or apps on your mobile phone.

    Have you used telephone banking in the past 12 months, either with a landline phone or your mobile phone?

    a. Yes

    b. No

[IF Q14=A; NUMBER BOX; RANGE: 0-99]

15. In the past **month**, about how many times have you used **telephone banking** to access your account? If none enter "0". _____times in the past month

[DISPLAY] [SAME AS S16674]

In this section we'll ask a few questions about your use of the Internet. Right now we are just interested in your use of the Internet **on a computer** (desktop, laptop) or **tablet**. Later on we will ask about use of the Internet on mobile phones.

[SP]

17. Do you currently have regular access to the internet, either at your home or outside your home (e.g., at school, work, public library, etc.) that is not provided by GfK, formerly Knowledge Networks?

    a. Yes

    b. No

[SP]

18. Which of the following best describes how easy it is for you to access the Internet on a desktop, laptop, or tablet (e.g., iPad)?

    a. Access is almost always available.

    b. Access is not always available, but is available at locations that are convenient for me (e.g., home, work, school).

    c. Access is available only at locations that require extra effort or planning to get to.

[SP, IF Q1=A]

19. **Online banking** involves checking your account balance and recent transactions, transferring money, paying bills, or conducting other related transactions with your bank or credit union using the Internet.

    Have you used online banking on a desktop, laptop, or tablet (e.g., iPad) computer in the past 12 months?

    a. Yes

    b. No

[IF Q19=A; NUMBER BOX; RANGE: 0-99]

20. In the past **month**, about how many times have you used online banking on a desktop, laptop, or tablet (e.g., iPad) computer? If none enter "0".
    _____times in the past month

Screener Question on Mobile Phone Usage

[DISPLAY][SHOW ON SAME SCREEN AS Q18]

In this section we would like to ask you about your use of mobile phones (cell phones).

[SP, PROMPT, TERMINATE IF SKIPPED]

21. Do you own or have regular access to a mobile phone (cell phone)?

    a. Yes ◆ **[MOBILE = "YES"]**

    b. No ◆ **[MOBILE = "NO"]**

DOV: MOBILE

1: "YES"

2: "NO"

[SP, IF MOBILE = "YES"]

22. A **smartphone** is a mobile phone with features that may enable it to access the web, send e-mails, download apps, and interact with computers. Smartphones include the iPhone, BlackBerry, as well as Android and Windows Mobile-powered devices.

    Is your mobile phone a smartphone?

    a. Yes

    b. No

[SP, IF Q22 = A]

23. Which type of smartphone do you have?

    a. Android

    b. BlackBberry

    c. iPhone

    d. Windows Mobile

    e. Amazon Fire

    f. Other

    g. Don't know

[SP, IF MOBILE = "YES"]

24. How confident are you in your ability to understand and navigate the technology and features of your mobile phone?

    a. Very confident

    b. Somewhat confident

    c. Not confident

[SP, IF Q22 = A]

25. Do you password protect your smartphone? Please count using a PIN, drawing a pattern, fingerprint or facial recognition, and other methods of securing your phone as password protection.

    a. Yes

    b. No

[SP, IF MOBILE= "YES"]

27. Which of the following best describes how easy it is for you to access the internet on your mobile phone through either WiFi or a wireless network (3G, 4G, LTE)?

  a. Access is almost always available.

  b. Access is not always available, but is available at locations that are convenient for me (e.g., home, work, school).

  c. Access is available only at locations that require extra effort or planning to get to.

  d. Access is not available.

  e. I do not need access to the Internet on my mobile phone.

Mobile Banking Users

[MOBILE = "YES" AND Q1 =A]

[DISPLAY; SHOW ON THE SAME SCREEN AS Q28 and Q29]

Mobile banking uses a mobile phone to access your bank or credit union account. This can be done either by accessing your bank or credit union's web page through the web browser on your mobile phone, via text messaging, or by using an app downloaded to your mobile phone.

[SP, MOBILE = "YES" AND Q1 =A; SHOW ON THE SAME SCREEN AS Q29]

28. Does your bank or credit union offer mobile banking?

  a. Yes

  b. No

  c. Don't know

[SP, MOBILE = "YES" AND Q1 =A; SHOW ON THE SAME SCREEN ASs Q28]

29. Have you used **mobile banking** in the past 12 months?

  a. Yes ◗ **[MOBILEBANK = "YES"]**

  b. No ◗ **[MOBILEBANK = "NO"]**

DOV: MOBILEBANK

1 "YES"

2 "NO"

[SP, IF MOBILE = "NO"]

30. Do you plan to use mobile banking in the next 12 months?

  a. Definitely will use

b. Probably will use

c. Probably will not use

d. Definitely will not use

[MOBILE = "YES" and Q1=A; GRID; SP ACROSS]

[SHOW THIS TEXT INSTEAD OF DEFAULT INSTRUCTIONS: Please answer yes or no to each option]

32. Using your **mobile phone**, have you done each of the following in the past 12 months.

	1 Yes	0 No
a. Downloaded your bank's mobile banking app on your mobile phone		
b. Checked an account balance or checked recent transactions		
c. Made a bill payment using your bank's online banking website or banking app		
d. Received an alert (e.g., a text message, push notification, or e-mail) from your bank		
e. Transferred money between your bank accounts		
f. Transferred money from your bank account to another person		
g. Deposited a check to your account electronically using your mobile phone camera		
h. Located the closest in-network ATM for your bank		

[IF MOBILEBANK= "YES"; NUMBER BOX; RANGE: 0-999]

33. In the past **month**, how many times have you personally used mobile banking? If none, enter "0." _____ times in the last month.

[SP, IF MOBILEBANK= "YES"; SHOW ON SAME SCREEN AS Q33]

34. When did you start using mobile banking?

a. In the last 6 months

b. 6 to 12 months ago

c. 1 to 2 years ago

d. More than 2 years ago

e. I don't remember

[SP, IF MOBILEBANK= "YES"]

35. What was the **main** reason why you started using mobile banking when you did?

a. I got a smartphone

b. My bank started offering the service

c. There is no bank branch or ATM near my home or work

d. I became comfortable with the security of mobile banking

e. I liked the convenience of mobile banking

f. To receive fraud alerts or check my account for fraudulent transactions

g. Other (please specify):**[TXT]**_____

Mobile Payments Users

[MOBILE = "YES"]

[DISPLAY; SHOW ON SAME SCREEN AS Q36]

Mobile payments are purchases, bill payments, charitable donations, payments to another person, or any other payments made using a mobile phone. You can do this either by accessing a web page through the web browser on your mobile device, by sending a text message (SMS), or by using a downloadable app on your mobile device. The amount of the payment may be applied to your phone bill (for example, Red Cross text message donation), charged to your credit card, deducted from a prepaid card, or withdrawn directly from your bank account.

[SP, MOBILE = "YES"]

36. Have you made a mobile payment in the past 12 months?

a. Yes ◆ **[MOBILEPAY = "YES"]**

b. No ◆ **[MOBILEPAY = "NO"]**

DOV: MOBILEPAY

1 "YES"

2 "NO"

[SP, MOBILE = "YES"; GRID; SP ACROSS]

[SHOW THIS TEXT INSTEAD OF DEFAULT INSTRUCTIONS: Please answer yes or no to each option]

37. Using your **mobile phone**, have you done each of the following in the past 12 months?

PROGRAMMING NOTE: CODE "Yes" AS 1, "No" AS 0, AND REFUSED AS -1.

	1 Yes	0 No
a. Transferred money directly to another person's bank or other financial account within the United States (e.g., Paypal account)		
b. Send a remittance (used to send money to relatives or friends living outside the U.S through WesternUnion, USPS SureMoney, etc.)		
c. Received money from another person's bank or other financial account (e.g., Paypal account)		
d. Paid for a product or service at a store (including at gas pumps and for restaurant meals)		
e. Paid for parking, a taxi, or public transit using an app		
f. Paid bills online through a mobile web browser or app		
g. Made a payment using a text message (including charitable donation by text message)		
h. Used an app to receive loyalty or reward points		
i. Made an online purchase or in-app purchase (e.g., from amazon.com or bestbuy.com)		

[IF MOBILEPAY = "YES"; NUMBER BOX; RANGE: 0-99]

38. In the past **month**, how many times have you used your mobile phone to make any type of mobile payment? If none, please enter "0." _____times in the last month.

[IF Q37d="YES"; GRID; SP ACROSS; SHOW ON SAME SCREEN AS Q40]

[SHOW THIS TEXT INSTEAD OF DEFAULT INSTRUCTIONS: Please answer yes or no to each option]

39. When you have used your mobile phone to pay for something **at a store in the past 12 months**, have you used your phone in each of these different ways?

    PROGRAMMING NOTE: CODE "Yes" AS 1, "No" AS 0, AND REFUSED AS -1.

	1 Yes	0 No
a. Waved or tapped my mobile phone to pay at check out (e.g., Google Wallet or Apple Pay)		
b. Scanned a barcode or QR code using your mobile phone to make a mobile payment (e.g., Starbucks app)		
c. Used a mobile app that doesn't require tapping the phone to pay at check out or scanning a barcode to pay for a purchase (e.g., Square Wallet)		
d. Other (please specify): **[txt]**_____		

[IF Q37d = "YES"; NUMBER BOX; RANGE: 0-99; SHOW ON SAME SCREEN AS Q39]

40. In the past **month**, about how many times have you used your mobile phone to pay for a product or service at a store? If none, please enter "0." _____times in the last month.

[MP, IF MOBILEPAY = "YES"]

41. When making mobile payments, which of the following payment methods do you use?

   a. Credit card

   b. Debit card

   c. Prepaid debit card

   d. Bank account

   e. Charge to your phone bill

   f. Account at a non-financial institution (e.g., PayPal)

   g. Other (please specify):**[TXT]**_____

[MP, IF MOBILEPAY = "YES" AND Q22= A]

42. Have you used any of the following mobile payment services in the past 12 months?

   a. Starbucks mobile payments

   b. Google Wallet

   c. Square Wallet

   d. Apple Pay

   e. Deluxe eCheck

   f. Amazon's Firefly

   g. CardNay

   h. PayPal

   i. LevelUp

   j. Dwolla

   k. Softcard

   l. Tabbedout

[SP, IF MOBILEPAY= "YES"; SHOW ON SAME SCREEN AS Q44]

43. When did you start using mobile payments?

   a. In the last 6 months

   b. 6 to 12 months ago

   c. 1 to 2 years ago

   d. More than 2 years ago

   e. I don't remember

[SP, IF MOBILEPAY= "YES"; SHOW ON SAME SCREEN AS Q43]

44. What was the **main** reason why you started using mobile payments when you did?

   a. I got a smartphone

   b. The ability to make mobile payments became available

   c. I became comfortable with the security of mobile payments

   d. I liked the convenience of mobile payments

   e. A store I visit started offering the service

   f. To take advantage of loyalty or rewards points and discounts

   g. Other (please specify):**[TXT]**_____

Non-Mobile Banking Users

[IF MOBILEBANK="NO" and Q28 = A]

[DISPLAY; SHOW ON SAME PAGE AS Q45]

We would like to ask you about some of your reasons for not using mobile banking.

[IF MOBILEBANK= "NO" AND MOBILE= "YES" AND Q28 = A]

[GRID; SP ACROSS; SHOW ON SAME PAGE AS DISPLAY]

[SHOW THIS TEXT INSTEAD OF DEFAULT INSTRUCTIONS: Please answer yes or no to each option**]**

45. Please tell us if each of the reasons below are why you do not use mobile banking.

    PROGRAMMING NOTE: CODE "Yes" AS 1, "No" AS 0, AND REFUSED AS -1.

	1 Yes	0 No
a. I'm concerned about the security of mobile banking		
b. My banking needs are being met without mobile banking		
c. I don't see any reason to use mobile banking		
d. The mobile phone screen is too small		
e. I don't have a smartphone		
f. My bank charges a fee for using mobile banking		
g. I don't do the banking in my household		
h. I don't trust the technology		
i. It's too difficult to use mobile banking		

[SP, IF Q45a = "Yes"]

46. You mentioned that security was one of your top concerns with mobile banking; which one of the following security aspects are you **most** concerned with?

   a. My phone getting hacked

   b. Someone using my phone without permission to access my account

   c. Someone intercepting my data

   d. Losing my phone or having my phone stolen

   e. Malware or viruses being installed on my phone

   f. Companies misusing my personal information

g. All of the above

h. Other (please specify):**[TXT]**_____

[MP, IF MOBILEBANK= "NO" AND Q28=A]

47. Assuming that the concerns that you have about using mobile banking were addressed, would you be interested in doing any of the following activities with your mobile phone?

    a. Download your bank's mobile banking app

    b. Check an account balance or check recent transactions

    c. Make bill payments using your bank's online banking website or app

    d. Receive alerts (e.g., text message, push notification, or e-mail) from your bank

    e. Deposit a check electronically using your mobile phone camera

    f. Transfer money between your bank accounts

    g. Transfer money from your bank account to another person

    h. Locate the closest in-network ATM or branch for your bank

    i. None, I don't want to use mobile banking **[Exclusive]**

[MP, IF Q28=B OR Q28=C]

48. You mentioned that your bank does not offer mobile banking or you are not sure if you bank offers it. If your bank or credit union were to offer mobile banking, would you be interested in doing any of the following activities with your mobile phone?

    a. Download your bank's mobile banking app

    b. Check an account balance or check recent transactions

    c. Make bill payments using your bank's online banking website or app

    d. Receive alerts (e.g., text message, push notification, or e-mail) from your bank

    e. Deposit a check electronically using your mobile phone camera

    f. Transfer money between your bank accounts

    g. Transfer money from your bank account to another person

    h. Locate the closest in-network ATM or branch for your bank

    i. None, I don't want to use mobile banking **[Exclusive]**

Non-Mobile Payments Users

[IF MOBILEPAY = "NO"]

[DISPLAY; shown on the same page as Q49]

We would like to ask you about some of your reasons for not using mobile payments

[IF MOBILEPAY = "NO" AND MOBILE = "YES"]

[GRID; SP ACROSS]

[SHOW THIS TEXT INSTEAD OF DEFAULT INSTRUCTIONS: Please answer yes or no to each option]

49. Please tell us if any of the reasons below are why you do not use mobile payments.

    PROGRAMMING NOTE: CODE "Yes" AS 1, "No" AS 0, AND REFUSED AS -1.

	1 Yes	0 No
a. I'm concerned about the security of mobile payments		
b. It's easier to pay with cash or a credit/debit card		
c. I don't see any benefit from using mobile payments		
d. The places I shop don't accept mobile payments		
e. I don't have the necessary feature on my phone		
f. I don't trust the technology		
g. It's difficult or time consuming to set up or use mobile payments		
h. I don't need to make any payments or someone else pays the bills		
i. I don't really understand all the different mobile payment options		

[SP, IF Q49a = "YES"]

50. You mentioned that security was one of your top concerns with mobile payments; which **one** of these security aspects are you most concerned with?

    a. My phone getting hacked

    b. Someone intercepting my payment information or other data

    c. Losing my phone or having my phone stolen

    d. Malware or viruses being installed on my phone

    e. Companies misusing my personal information

    f. All of the above

    g. Other (please specify):**[txt]**_____

[MP, IF MOBILEPAY = "NO"]

51. Assuming that the reason(s) why you do not currently use mobile payments was addressed, would you be interested in doing any of the following activities with your mobile phone?

    a. Making payments to another person (e.g., friend, relative, babysitter) within the United States

    b. Transferring money to someone in another country

    c. Using my mobile phone to pay for purchases at a store

    d. Paying for parking, a taxi, or public transit using an app

e. Paying bills online through a mobile web browser or app

f. Using your mobile phone as a "virtual wallet" to replace some cards in your wallet

g. Making an online or in-app purchase (e.g., from amazon.com or bestbuy.com)

h. Receiving money from another person's bank or other financial account (e.g., Paypal account)

i. Receiving/using coupons and/or reward points on your phone

j. None, I don't want to use mobile payments **[Exclusive]**

[SP, IF Q37d= "NO"]

52. You indicated that you have not made a mobile payment in a store in the last 12 months. Do you plan to use your mobile phone to make a payment in a store in the next 12 months?

    a. Definitely will use

    b. Probably will use

    c. Probably will not use

    d. Definitely will not use

Mobile Financial Services Security Questions

[MOBILE = "YES" FOR QUESTIONS 53 THROUGH 54]

[DISPLAY, SHOW IT ON THE SAME SCREEN WITH Q53 TO Q54]

Please rate your perception of the level of security for each of the following mobile financial services from Very Safe to Very Unsafe.

[SP, SHOW ON THE SAME SCREEN AS Q54]

53. How safe do you believe people's personal information is when they use mobile banking?

    a. Very safe

    b. Somewhat safe

    c. Somewhat unsafe

    d. Very unsafe

    e. Don't know

[SP, SHOW ON THE SAME SCREEN AS Q53]

54. How safe do you believe people's personal information is when they use a mobile phone to pay for a purchase at a store?

    a. Very safe

    b. Somewhat safe

    c. Somewhat unsafe

    d. Very unsafe

    e. Don't know

[SP, GRID; IF MOBILE = "YES"]

55. Would you like to or do you already use your mobile phone for any of the following purposes?

	1 I already do	2 I would like to	3 I am unlikely to
a. Track your finances, purchases, or expenses			
b. Organize, track and store gift cards, memberships, loyalty and reward points			
c. Compare prices when shopping			
d. Receive and manage discount offers and coupons			
e. Receive offers and promotions based on your location			

[SP, IF Q22=A]

[DISPLAY][SHOW ON THE SAME SCREEN AS Q56 AND Q57]

For the following two questions please rate how much you agree or disagree with the statement on a scale from strongly agree to strongly disagree.

[SP, IF Q22=A]

[SHOW ON THE SAME SCREEN AS Q57]

56. I am willing to allow my mobile phone to provide my location to companies I shop with regularly so that they can offer me discounts, promotions, or services based on where I am.

    a. Strongly agree

    b. Agree

    c. Disagree

    d. Strongly disagree

[SP, IF Q22=A]

[SHOW ON THE SAME SCREEN AS Q56]

57. I am willing to allow my mobile phone to provide personal information such as my sex, age, friends, and shopping history to companies I shop with regularly so that they can offer me targeted discounts, promotions, or services.

    a. Strongly agree

    b. Agree

    c. Disagree

    d. Strongly disagree

Shopping Behavior Questions

[IF MOBILE= "YES" AND Q22=A]

[DISPLAY][SHOW ON SAME SCREEN AS Q58]

In this section we would like to ask you about your shopping habits.

[SP, IF MOBILE= "YES" AND Q22=A][SHOW ON SAME SCREEN AS Q59]

58. Have you ever used your mobile phone to comparison shop over the Internet while at a retail store?

    a. Yes

    b. No

[SP, IF MOBILE= "YES" AND Q22=A][SHOW ON SAME SCREEN AS Q58]

59. Have you ever used a barcode scanning app on your mobile phone while shopping at a retail store to find the best price for an item?

    a. Yes

    b. No

[SP, IF Q58 = A OR Q59 = A]

61. Has using your mobile phone to compare prices while you were shopping at a retail store ever changed where you made your purchase?

    a. Yes

    b. No

[SP, IF MOBILE= "YES" AND Q22=A][SHOW ON SAME SCREEN AS Q62]

60. Have you ever scanned a QR code (similar to a barcode) in a retail store, newspaper, magazine, or billboard advertisement to obtain information about a product on your mobile phone?

    a. Yes

    b. No

[SP, IF MOBILE= "YES" AND Q22=A][SHOW ON SAME SCREEN AS Q60]

62. Have you ever used your mobile phone to browse product reviews or get product information while shopping at a retail store? This could be done by, for example, googling the product on your mobile browser or scanning a QR code.

    a. Yes

    b. No

[SP, IF Q62 = A]

63. Has reading product reviews on your mobile phone while shopping at a retail store ever changed which item you ended up purchasing?

    a. Yes

    b. No

[SP, IF MOBILEBANK = "YES" AND Q22 = A]

64. In the past 12 months, have you used your mobile phone to check your account balance or available credit before making a large purchase?

    a. Yes

    b. No

[SP, IF Q64 = A]

65. Thinking of the most recent time that you checked your account balance or available credit before making a large purchase, did you decide not to buy that particular item because of the amount of money left in your account or the amount of your available credit?

    a. Yes

    b. No

Financial Management (Saving, Budgeting) Questions

[MP, IF Q32 = D]

66. You previously mentioned that you receive text message, push notifications, or e-mail alerts from your financial institution. Do you receive each of the following kinds of alerts?

    a. Low balance

    b. Payment due

    c. Saving reminders

    d. Fraud

    e. Credit card balance

    f. Deposit or withdrawal

    g. Statement available notification

    h. Other (please specify):**[txt]**_____

[MP, IF Q66= A]

67. Thinking of the most recent low-balance alert you received, which of the following actions did you take after receiving the alert?

    a. Transferred money into the account with the low balance from another account

b. Deposited money into the account with the low balance

c. Reduced my spending

d. None of the above **[Exclusive]**

Table C.1. Do you or does your spouse/partner currently have some type of bank or credit union account such as a checking, savings, or money market account?
Percent, except as noted

Q1	
Refused	0.3
Yes	87.0
No	12.7
Number of respondents	2,925

Table C.2. Have you or your spouse/partner ever had some type of bank or credit union account such as a checking, savings, or money market account?
Percent, except as noted

Q2	
Refused	1.2
Yes	30.5
No	68.3
Number of respondents	233

Table C.3. Have you used a prepaid debit card in the past 12 months?

Q4a	
Refused	0.1
Yes	19.8
No	80.1
Number of respondents	2,925

Table C.4. Have you sent a remittance in the past 12 months?
Percent, except as noted

Q5	
Refused	0.3
Yes	7.4
No	92.3
Number of respondents	2,925

Table C.5. In the past 12 months, have you used a money order, check cashing service, pawn shop loan, auto title loan, paycheck advance/deposit advance, or a payday loan?
Percent, except as noted

Q5a	
Refused	0.3
Yes	16.7
No	83.0
Number of respondents	2,925

Table C.6. What are the three main ways you (or your spouse/partner) interact with your bank or credit union when you use your accounts? Use number 1 for most often, 2 for 2nd most often, 3 for 3rd most often used.
Percent, except as noted

Q16	1	2	3
Refused/no rank	0.8	6.8	16.9
ATM/cash machine	30.0	25.1	17.7
A teller in person at a branch	25.9	24.6	23.9
Mail	1.8	4.1	7.7
Phone – talking or using touchtone service	2.2	8.6	12.2
Over the Internet using a computer/tablet	30.0	20.6	12.0
Mobile phone app, mobile web browser, or SMS/text message	7.5	8.7	7.4
Family member, friend, or neighbor does the banking for me	1.5	1.4	2.0
Other	0.4	0.3	0.3
Number of respondents	2,685		

Table C.7. Have you visited a bank branch and spoken with a teller or a bank employee in the past 12 months?
Percent, except as noted

Q6	
Refused	0.2
Yes	87.3
No	12.5
Number of respondents	2,685

Table C.8. In the past month, about how many times have you visited a branch and spoken with a teller or a bank employee? If none enter "0".

	Q7
Refused (percent)	0.3
Total respondents with zero uses (percent)	23.3
Mean number of uses (at least one use)	2.9
Median number of uses (at least one use)	2.0
Number of respondents	2,389

Table C.12. In the past month, about how many times have you used an ATM for banking transactions? If none enter "0".

	Q11
Refused (percent)	0.6
Total respondents with zero uses (percent)	15.0
Mean number of uses (at least one use)	3.9
Median number of uses (at least one use)	3.0
Number of respondents	1,977

Table C.9. Which of the following best describes the location of your bank or credit union branch that you typically visit when you need to speak with a teller or bank employee?

Percent, except as noted

	Q8
Refused	0.2
I visit a branch close to my home, work, school, or other place I go to frequently	85.0
I must go out of my way or travel for a while to visit a branch	7.0
I am not able to visit a branch because my bank does not have a branch in my area	2.3
I do not need to visit a branch	5.5
Number of respondents	2,685

Table C.13. Which of the following best describes the location of the ATM that you typically use for banking transactions?

Percent, except as noted

	Q12
Refused	0.4
I use an ATM close to my home, work, school, or other place I go to frequently	75.0
I must go out of my way or travel for a while to access the ATM	4.0
I am not able to use an ATM for banking transactions because there is not an ATM in my area	0.6
I do not use an ATM	20.0
Number of respondents	2,685

Table C.10. About how long does it take you to travel to the branch you typically visit (one way)?

	Q9
Refused (percent)	0.2
Mean number of minutes	10.3
Median number of minutes	8.0
Number of respondents	2,484

Table C.14. About how long does it take you to travel to the ATM you typically use (one way)?

	Q13
Refused (percent)	0.5
Mean number of minutes	8.4
Median number of minutes	5.0
Number of respondents	2,073

Table C.11. Have you used an ATM for any banking transactions in the past 12 months?

Percent, except as noted

	Q10
Refused	0.2
Yes	75.2
No	24.6
Number of respondents	2,685

Table C.15. Have you used telephone banking in the past 12 months, either with a land-line phone or your mobile phone?

Percent, except as noted

	Q14
Refused	0.3
Yes	32.7
No	67.0
Number of respondents	2,685

Table C.16. In the past month, about how many times have you used telephone banking to access your account? If none enter "0".

	Q15
Refused (percent)	0.3
Total respondents with zero uses (percent)	27.1
Mean number of uses (at least one use)	3.8
Median number of uses (at least one use)	2.0
Number of respondents	**815**

Table C.17. Do you currently have regular access to the Internet, either at your home or outside your home (e.g., at school, work, public library, etc.) that is not provided by GfK, formerly Knowledge Networks?
Percent, except as noted

	Q17
Refused	0.4
Yes	88.0
No	11.6
Number of respondents	**2,925**

Table C.18. Which of the following best describes how easy it is for you to access the Internet on a desktop, laptop, or tablet (e.g., iPad)?
Percent, except as noted

	Q18
Refused	1.4
Access is almost always available	83.5
Access is not always available, but is available at locations that are convenient for me (e.g., home, work, school)	11.1
Access is available only at locations that require extra effort or planning to get to	4.0
Number of respondents	**2,925**

Table C.19. Have you used online banking on a desktop, laptop, or tablet (e.g., iPad) computer in the past 12 months?
Percent, except as noted

	Q19
Refused	0.6
Yes	73.7
No	25.7
Number of respondents	**2,685**

Table C.20. In the past month, about how many times have you used online banking on a desktop, laptop, or tablet (e.g., iPad) computer? If none enter "0".

	Q20
Refused (percent)	0.1
Total respondents with zero uses (percent)	5.0
Mean number of uses (at least one use)	9.1
Median number of uses (at least one use)	5.0
Number of respondents	**2,026**

Table C.21. Do you own or have regular access to a mobile phone (cell phone)?
Percent, except as noted

	Q21
Yes	86.8
No	13.2
Number of respondents	**2,925**

Table C.22. Is your mobile phone a smartphone?
Percent, except as noted

	Q22
Refused	0.3
Yes	70.9
No	28.8
Number of respondents	**2,603**

Table C.23. Which type of smartphone do you have?
Percent, except as noted

	Q23
Android	47.7
BlackBerry	1.1
iPhone	44.1
Windows Mobile	1.8
Amazon Fire	0.3*
Other	3.2
Don't know	1.9
Number of respondents	**1,775**

* Fewer than 10 responses were received for this option.

Table C.24. How confident are you in your ability to understand and navigate the technology and features of your mobile phone?

Percent, except as noted

Q24	
Refused	0.5
Very confident	54.0
Somewhat confident	33.5
Not confident	12.0
Number of respondents	**2,603**

Table C.25. Do you password protect your smartphone?

Percent, except as noted

Q25	
Refused	0.6
Yes	69.2
No	30.2
Number of respondents	**1,775**

Table C.26. Which of the following best describes how easy it is for you to access the Internet on your mobile phone through either WiFi or a wireless network (3G, 4G, LTE)?

Percent, except as noted

Q27	
Refused	0.7
Access is almost always available	63.0
Access is not always available, but is available at locations that are convenient for me (e.g., home, work, school)	9.1
Access is available only at locations that require extra effort or planning to get to	1.3
Access is not available	7.4
I do not need access to the Internet on my mobile phone	18.6
Number of respondents	**2,603**

Table C.27. Does your bank or credit union offer mobile banking?

Percent, except as noted

Q28	
Refused	0.4
Yes	74.0
No	4.1
Don't know	21.5
Number of respondents	**2,437**

Table C.28. Have you used mobile banking in the past 12 months?

Percent, except as noted

Q29	
Refused	1.2
Yes	38.7
No	60.1
Number of respondents	**2,437**

Table C.29. Do you plan to use mobile banking in the next 12 months?

Percent, except as noted

Q30	
Definitely will use	1.2
Probably will use	9.8
Probably will not use	45.4
Definitely will not use	43.7
Number of respondents	**1,584**

Table C.30. Using your mobile phone, have you done each of the following in the past 12 months?

Percent, except as noted

Q32	
No/refused to all	46.6
Downloaded your bank's mobile banking app on your mobile phone	30.2
Checked an account balance or checked recent transactions	44.9
Made a bill payment using your bank's online banking website or banking app	21.0
Received an alert (e.g., a text message, push notification, or e-mail) from your bank	28.5
Transferred money between your bank accounts	26.8
Transferred money from your bank account to another person	10.4
Deposited a check to your account electronically using your mobile phone camera	20.1
Located the closest in-network ATM or branch for your bank	20.2
Number of respondents	**2,437**

Note: This question was asked of those with a mobile phone and a bank account and includes those who did not identify themselves as having used mobile banking in the previous 12 months.

Table C.31. In the past month, about how many times have you personally used mobile banking?

Q33	
Refused (percent)	3.5
Total respondents with zero uses (percent)	6.4
Mean number of uses (at least one use)	10.0
Median number of uses (at least one use)	5.0
Number of respondents	**829**

Table C.32. When did you start using mobile banking?

Percent, except as noted

Q34	
Refused	5.1
In the last 6 months	14.6
6 to 12 months ago	11.6
1 to 2 years ago	27.6
More than 2 years ago	36.3
I don't remember	4.7
Number of respondents	**829**

Table C.33. What was the main reason why you started using mobile banking when you did?

Percent, except as noted

Q35	
Refused	0.1
I got a smartphone	32.5
My bank started offering the service	19.8
There is no bank branch or ATM near my home or work	3.5
I became comfortable with the security of mobile banking	5.7
I liked the convenience of mobile banking	34.6
To receive fraud alerts or check my account for fraudulent transactions	0.9*
Other (please specify):	3.1
Number of respondents	**829**

* Fewer than 10 responses were received for this option.

Table C.34. Have you made a mobile payment in the past 12 months?
Percent, except as noted

Q36	
Refused	0.7
Yes	21.7
No	77.6
Number of respondents	2,603

Table C.35. Using your mobile phone, have you done each of the following in the past 12 months?
Percent, except as noted

Q37	
No/refused to all	64.5
Transferred money directly to another person's bank or other financial account within the United States (e.g., Paypal account)	10.8
Send a remittance (used to send money to relatives or friends living outside the U.S through WesternUnion, USPS SureMoney, etc.)	2.2
Received money from another person's bank or other financial account (e.g., Paypal account)	9.9
Paid for a product or service at a store (including at gas pumps and for restaurant meals)	12.9
Paid for parking, a taxi, or public transit using an app	4.8
Paid bills online through a mobile web browser or app	19.7
Made a payment using a text message (including charitable donation by text message)	2.8
Used an app to receive loyalty or reward points	12.0
Made an online or in-app purchase (e.g., from amazon.com or bestbuy.com)	20.9
Number of respondents	2,603

Note: This question was asked of those with a mobile phone and includes those who did not identify themselves as having used mobile payments in the previous 12 months.

Table C.36. In the past month, about how many times have you used your mobile phone to make any type of mobile payment? If none please enter "0".

Q38	
Refused (percent)	1.6
Total respondents with zero uses (percent)	26.6
Mean number of uses (at least one use)	4.9
Median number of uses (at least one use)	3.0
Number of respondents	455

Table C.37. When you have used your mobile phone to pay for something at a store in the past 12 months, have you used your phone in each of these different ways?
Percent, except as noted

Q39	
No/refused to all	57.8
Waved or tapped my mobile phone to pay at check out (e.g., Google Wallet or Apple Pay)	11.6
Scanned a barcode or QR code using your mobile phone to make a mobile payment (e.g., Starbucks app)	28.6
Used a mobile app that doesn't require tapping the phone to pay at check out or scanning a barcode to pay for a purchase (e.g., Square Wallet)	18.6
Other	1.7
Number of respondents	283

Table C.38. In the past month, about how many times have you used your mobile phone to pay for a product or service at a store? If none please enter "0".

Q40	
Refused (percent)	12.0
Total respondents with zero uses (percent)	50.1
Mean number of uses (at least one use)	4.7
Median number of uses (at least one use)	3.0
Number of respondents	283

Table C.39. When making mobile payments, which of the following payment methods do you use?

Percent, except as noted

Q41	
Refused	2.0
Credit card	51.2
Debit card	55.0
Prepaid debit card	7.6
Bank account	40.7
Charge to your phone bill	4.2
Account at a non-financial institution (e.g., PayPal)	15.4
Other	3.1
Number of respondents	455

Table C.40. Have you used any of the following mobile payment services in the past 12 months?

Percent, except as noted

Q42	
Refused	42.3
Starbucks mobile payments	10.9
Google Wallet	9.0
Square Wallet	1.6*
Apple Pay	4.9
Deluxe eCheck	0.9*
Amazon Firefly	2.9*
CardNav	1.1*
PayPal	43.1
LevelUp	0.8*
Dwolla	0.0
Softcard	0.6*
Tabbedout	0.0
Number of respondents	428

* Fewer than 10 responses were received for this option.

Table C.41. When did you start using mobile payments?

Percent, except as noted

Q43	
Refused	2.5
In the last 6 months	15.9
6 to 12 months ago	13.1
1 to 2 years ago	20.9
More than 2 years ago	25.6
I don't remember	21.9
Number of respondents	455

Table C.42. What was the main reason why you started using mobile payments when you did?

Percent, except as noted

Q44	
Refused	4.5
I got a smartphone	33.7
The ability to make mobile payments became available	15.5
I became comfortable with the security of mobile payments	8.7
I liked the convenience of mobile payments	29.1
A store I visit started offering the service	2.3
To take advantage of loyalty or rewards points and discounts	2.6
Other (please specify):	3.5
Number of respondents	455

Table C.43. Please tell us if each of the reasons below are why you do not use mobile banking.

Percent, except as noted

Q45	
No/refused to all	4.8
I'm concerned about the security of mobile banking	62.1
My banking needs are being met without mobile banking	85.8
I don't see any reason to use mobile banking	73.0
The mobile phone screen is too small	39.4
I don't have a smartphone	32.3
My bank charges a fee for using mobile banking	6.5
I don't do the banking in my household	12.5
I don't trust the technology	34.3
It's too difficult to use mobile banking	19.9
Number of respondents	945

Table C.44. You mentioned that security was one of your top concerns with mobile banking; which one of the following security aspects are you most concerned with?
Percent, except as noted

Q46	
Refused	0.5
My phone getting hacked	17.1
Someone using my phone without permission to access my account	4.1
Someone intercepting my data	22.3
Losing my phone or having my phone stolen	8.9
Malware or viruses being installed on my phone	1.8
Companies misusing my personal information	2.0*
All of the above	42.9
Other (please specify):	0.4*
Number of respondents	600

* Fewer than 10 responses were received for this option.

Table C.45. Assuming that the concerns that you have about using mobile banking were addressed, would you be interested in doing any of the following activities with your mobile phone?
Percent, except as noted

Q47	
Refused	0.5
Download your bank's mobile banking app	21.3
Check an account balance or check recent transactions	32.2
Make bill payments using your bank's online banking website or app	14.9
Receive alerts (e.g., text message, push notification, or e-mail) from your bank	19.3
Deposit a check electronically using your mobile phone camera	17.4
Transfer money between your bank accounts	20.3
Transfer money from your bank account to another person	11.3
Locate the closest in-network ATM or branch for your bank	18.2
None, I don't want to use mobile banking	59.2
Number of respondents	945

Table C.46. You mentioned that your bank does not offer mobile banking or you are not sure if your bank offers it. If your bank or credit union were to offer mobile banking, would you be interested in doing any of the following activities with your mobile phone?
Percent, except as noted

Q48	
Refused	0.3
Download your bank's mobile banking app	8.1
Check an account balance or check recent transactions	15.0
Make bill payments using your bank's online banking website or app	6.2
Receive alerts (e.g., text message, push notification, or e-mail) from your bank	7.1
Deposit a check electronically using your mobile phone camera	6.7
Transfer money between your bank accounts	6.6
Transfer money from your bank account to another person	3.4
Locate the closest in-network ATM or branch for your bank	6.9
None, I don't want to use mobile banking	79.0
Number of respondents	650

Table C.47. Please tell us if any of the reasons below are why you do not use mobile payments.
Percent, except as noted

Q49	
No/refused to all	8.4
I'm concerned about the security of mobile payments	59.4
It's easier to pay with cash or a credit/debit card	75.3
I don't see any benefit from using mobile payments	59.4
The places I shop don't accept mobile payments	23.2
I don't have the necessary feature on my phone	37.0
I don't trust the technology	41.0
It's difficult or time consuming to set up or use mobile payments	31.0
I don't need to make any payments or someone else pays the bills	23.4
I don't really understand all the different mobile payment options	31.2
Number of respondents	2,137

Table C.48. You mentioned that security was one of your top concerns with mobile payments; which one of these security aspects are you most concerned with?

Percent, except as noted

Q50	
Refused	0.2
My phone getting hacked	13.1
Someone intercepting my payment information or other data	20.7
Losing my phone or having my phone stolen	10.0
Malware or viruses being installed on my phone	1.7
Companies misusing my personal information	2.7
All of the above	51.0
Other (please specify):	0.6*
Number of respondents	1,286

* Fewer than 10 responses were received for this option.

Table C.49. Assuming that the reason(s) why you do not currently use mobile payments was addressed, would you be interested in doing any of the following activities with your mobile phone?

Percent, except as noted

Q51	
Refused	1.0
Making payments to another person (e.g., friend, relative, babysitter) within the United States	11.2
Transferring money to someone in another country	4.3
Using my mobile phone to pay for purchases at a store	17.7
Paying for parking, a taxi, or public transit using an app	12.3
Paying bills online through a mobiel web browser or app	15.0
Using your mobile phone as a "virtual wallet" to replace some cards in your wallet	12.5
Making an online or in-app purchase (e.g., from amazon.com or bestbuy.com)	14.7
Receiving money from another person's bank or other financial account (e.g., Paypal account)	11.6
Receiving/using coupons and/or reward points on your phone	19.8
None, I don't want to use mobile payments	65.5
Number of respondents	2,137

Table C.50. You indicated that you have not made a mobile payment in a store in the last 12 months. Do you plan to use your mobile phone to make a payment in a store in the next 12 months?

Percent, except as noted

Q52	
Refused	0.2
Definitely will use	3.6
Probably will use	11.2
Probably will not use	37.7
Definitely will not use	47.2
Number of respondents	2,300

Table C.51. How safe do you believe people's personal information is when they use mobile banking?

Percent, except as noted

Q53	
Refused	0.9
Very safe	6.7
Somewhat safe	33.6
Somewhat unsafe	24.7
Very unsafe	19.0
Don't know	15.1
Number of respondents	2,603

Table C.52. How safe do you believe people's personal information is when they use a mobile phone to pay for a purchase at a store?

Percent, except as noted

Q54	
Refused	0.9
Very safe	5.2
Somewhat safe	29.7
Somewhat unsafe	27.8
Very unsafe	21.0
Don't know	15.4
Number of respondents	2,603

Table C.53. Would you like to or do you already use your mobile phone for any of the following purposes?

Percent, except as noted

Q55	Refused	I already do	I would like to	I am unlikely to
Track your finances, purchases or expenses	1.0	28.5	13.2	57.2
Organize, track and store gift cards, memberships, loyalty and reward points	1.2	13.3	19.3	66.3
Compare prices when shopping	1.2	29.7	24.3	44.8
Receive and manage discount offers and coupons	1.1	23.0	25.5	50.3
Receive offers and promotions based on your location	1.2	17.5	23.8	57.5
Number of respondents	2,603			

Table C.54. I am willing to allow my mobile phone to provide my location to companies I shop with regularly so that they can offer me discounts, promotions, or services based on where I am.

Percent, except as noted

Q56	
Refused	1.1
Strongly agree	6.2
Agree	33.5
Disagree	32.9
Strongly disagree	26.4
Number of respondents	1,775

Table C.55. I am willing to allow my mobile phone to provide personal information such as my sex, age, friends, and shopping history to companies I shop with regularly so that they can offer me targeted discounts, promotions, or services.

Percent, except as noted

Q57	
Refused	1.0
Strongly agree	3.4
Agree	19.4
Disagree	37.0
Strongly disagree	39.3
Number of respondents	1,775

Table C.56. Have you ever used your mobile phone to comparison shop over the Internet while at a retail store?

Percent, except as noted

Q58	
Refused	0.9
Yes	46.5
No	52.6
Number of respondents	1,775

Table C.57. Have you ever used a barcode scanning app on your mobile phone while shopping at a retail store to find the best price for an item?

Percent, except as noted

Q59	
Refused	0.8
Yes	32.8
No	66.4
Number of respondents	1,775

Table C.58. Has using your mobile phone to compare prices while you were shopping at a retail store ever changed where you made your purchase?

Percent, except as noted

Q61	
Refused	0.4
Yes	68.6
No	31.0
Number of respondents	894

Table C.59. Have you ever scanned a QR code (similar to a barcode) in a retail store, newspaper, magazine, or billboard advertisement to obtain information about a product on your mobile phone?

Percent, except as noted

Q60	
Refused	1.2
Yes	30.8
No	68.0
Number of respondents	1,775

Table C.60. Have you ever used your mobile phone to browse product reviews or get product information while shopping at a retail store? This could be done by, for example, googling the product on your mobile browser or scanning a QR code.

Percent, except as noted

Q62	
Refused	1.4
Yes	42.2
No	56.5
Number of respondents	1,775

Table C.61. Has reading product reviews on your mobile phone while shopping at a retail store ever changed which item you ended up purchasing?

Percent, except as noted

Q63	
Refused	0.1
Yes	78.7
No	21.3
Number of respondents	712

Table C.62. In the past 12 months, have you used your mobile phone to check your account balance or available credit before making a large purchase?

Percent, except as noted

Q64	
Refused	0.2
Yes	63.4
No	36.4
Number of respondents	798

Table C.63. Thinking of the most recent time that you checked your account balance or available credit before making a large purchase, did you decide not to buy that particular item because of the amount of money left in your account or the amount of your available credit?

Percent, except as noted

Q65	
Refused	0.7
Yes	53.1
No	46.2
Number of respondents	462

Table C.64. You previously mentioned that you receive text message, push notification, or e-mail alerts from your financial institution. Do you receive each of the following kinds of alerts?

Percent, except as noted

Q66	
Refused	1.9
Low balance	42.4
Payment due	32.8
Saving reminders	4.6
Fraud	32.2
Credit card balance	14.7
Deposit or withdrawal	36.7
Statement available notification	39.7
Other	7.1
Number of respondents	629

Table C.65. Thinking of the most recent low-balance alert you received, which of the following actions did you take after receiving the alert?

Percent, except as noted

Q67	
Refused	0.2
Transferred money into the account with the low balance from another account	41.0
Deposited money into the account with the low balance	29.7
Reduced my spending	28.2
None of the above	20.2
Number of respondents	256

Summary Statistics for Demographics

Table C.66. Summary statistics for demographics: Full sample	Weighted		Unweighted	
	Mean	Standard deviation	Mean	Standard deviation
Age	47.0650	17.2240	52.3371	16.9816
Male	0.4824	0.4998	0.5183	0.4998
Female	0.5176	0.4998	0.4817	0.4998
18–29	0.2140	0.4102	0.1323	0.3389
30–44	0.2532	0.4349	0.1993	0.3996
45–60	0.2684	0.4432	0.2882	0.4530
Ages over 60	0.2644	0.4411	0.3802	0.4855
Less than high school	0.1237	0.3293	0.0646	0.2459
High school degree	0.2963	0.4567	0.2745	0.4464
Some college	0.2874	0.4526	0.2868	0.4524
Bachelor's degree or higher	0.2925	0.4550	0.3740	0.4840
White, non-Hispanic	0.6552	0.4754	0.7665	0.4231
Black, non-Hispanic	0.1153	0.3195	0.0800	0.2713
Other, non-Hispanic	0.0777	0.2677	0.0687	0.2530
Hispanic	0.1518	0.3589	0.0848	0.2786
2 or more races, non-Hispanic	0.0128	0.1123	0.0294	0.1690
Less than $25,000	0.2164	0.4119	0.1590	0.3657
$25,000–$39,999	0.1543	0.3613	0.1398	0.3469
$40,000–$74,999	0.1651	0.3713	0.1689	0.3747
$75,000–$99,999	0.2306	0.4213	0.2537	0.4352
Greater than $100,000	0.2335	0.4231	0.2786	0.4484
Married	0.5105	0.5000	0.5959	0.4908
Not married	0.4895	0.5000	0.4041	0.4908
Metropolitan	0.8439	0.3630	0.8373	0.3692
Northeast	0.1821	0.3860	0.1867	0.3897
Midwest	0.2135	0.4098	0.2284	0.4199
South	0.3707	0.4831	0.3600	0.4801
West	0.2337	0.4233	0.2250	0.4176
Employed	0.5664	0.4957	0.5525	0.4973
Unemployed, in labor force	0.0850	0.2789	0.0547	0.2274
Not in labor force	0.3487	0.4766	0.3928	0.4885
Observations	2,925			

Table C.67. Summary statistics for demographics: All mobile phone users (feature and smartphone)	Weighted		Unweighted	
	Mean	Standard deviation	Mean	Standard deviation
Age	46.1954	16.9504	51.6815	16.8657
Male	0.4818	0.4998	0.5167	0.4998
Female	0.5182	0.4998	0.4833	0.4998
18–29	0.2226	0.4161	0.1364	0.3433
30–44	0.2656	0.4417	0.2098	0.4072
45–60	0.2692	0.4436	0.2908	0.4542
Ages over 60	0.2426	0.4287	0.3630	0.4810
Less than high school	0.1059	0.3078	0.0553	0.2286
High school degree	0.2838	0.4509	0.2620	0.4398
Some college	0.2945	0.4559	0.2897	0.4537
Bachelor's degree or higher	0.3158	0.4649	0.3930	0.4885
White, non-Hispanic	0.6664	0.4716	0.7722	0.4195
Black, non-Hispanic	0.1096	0.3125	0.0772	0.2670
Other, non-Hispanic	0.0747	0.2630	0.0676	0.2511
Hispanic	0.1492	0.3563	0.0830	0.2759
2 or more races, non-Hispanic	0.0108	0.1033	0.0288	0.1673
Less than $25,000	0.1839	0.3875	0.1348	0.3416
$25,000—$39,999	0.1499	0.3570	0.1348	0.3416
$40,000–$74,999	0.1697	0.3754	0.1690	0.3749
$75,000–$99,999	0.2408	0.4277	0.2647	0.4413
Greater than $100,000	0.2556	0.4363	0.2966	0.4568
Married	0.5300	0.4992	0.6135	0.4870
Not married	0.4700	0.4992	0.3865	0.4870
Metropolitan	0.8530	0.3542	0.8444	0.3625
Northeast	0.1898	0.3922	0.1894	0.3919
Midwest	0.2034	0.4026	0.2197	0.4142
South	0.3731	0.4837	0.3665	0.4819
West	0.2337	0.4232	0.2244	0.4172
Employed	0.6114	0.4875	0.5843	0.4929
Unemployed, in labor force	0.0782	0.2685	0.0515	0.2210
Not in labor force	0.3105	0.4628	0.3642	0.4813
Observations	2,603			

Table C.68. Summary statistics for demographics: Smartphone users	Weighted		Unweighted	
	Mean	Standard deviation	Mean	Standard deviation
Age	42.4617	15.4502	47.8068	16.0438
Male	0.4865	0.5000	0.5217	0.4997
Female	0.5135	0.5000	0.4783	0.4997
18–29	0.2652	0.4416	0.1707	0.3764
30–44	0.3223	0.4675	0.2642	0.4410
45–60	0.2531	0.4349	0.3020	0.4592
Ages over 60	0.1593	0.3661	0.2631	0.4404
Less than high school	0.0778	0.2679	0.0394	0.1947
High school degree	0.2611	0.4393	0.2287	0.4201
Some college	0.3023	0.4594	0.2946	0.4560
Bachelor's degree or higher	0.3588	0.4798	0.4372	0.4962
White, non-Hispanic	0.6403	0.4801	0.7487	0.4339
Black, non-Hispanic	0.1028	0.3037	0.0761	0.2652
Other, non-Hispanic	0.0847	0.2785	0.0744	0.2624
Hispanic	0.1723	0.3777	0.1008	0.3012
2 or more races, non-Hispanic	0.0098	0.0986	0.0270	0.1623
Less than $25,000	0.1376	0.3446	0.0969	0.2959
$25,000–$39,999	0.1347	0.3415	0.1149	0.3190
$40,000–$74,999	0.1739	0.3791	0.1645	0.3708
$75,000–$99,999	0.2489	0.4325	0.2659	0.4419
Greater than $100,000	0.3049	0.4605	0.3577	0.4795
Married	0.5431	0.4983	0.6248	0.4843
Not married	0.4569	0.4983	0.3752	0.4843
Metropolitan	0.8680	0.3386	0.8575	0.3497
Northeast	0.1836	0.3873	0.1803	0.3845
Midwest	0.1909	0.3931	0.2096	0.4071
South	0.3785	0.4851	0.3752	0.4843
West	0.2470	0.4314	0.2349	0.4241
Employed	0.6878	0.4635	0.6715	0.4698
Unemployed, in labor force	0.0803	0.2719	0.0552	0.2285
Not in labor force	0.2318	0.4221	0.2732	0.4457
Observations	1,775			

Table C.69. Summary statistics for demographics: Feature phone users	Weighted		Unweighted	
	Mean	Standard deviation	Mean	Standard deviation
Age	55.4315	16.9421	60.0537	15.5039
Male	0.4695	0.4994	0.5049	0.5003
Female	0.5305	0.4994	0.4951	0.5003
18–29	0.1166	0.3211	0.0622	0.2417
30–44	0.1272	0.3333	0.0927	0.2902
45–60	0.3081	0.4620	0.2659	0.4421
Ages over 60	0.4482	0.4976	0.5793	0.4940
Less than high school	0.1762	0.3813	0.0902	0.2867
High school degree	0.3403	0.4741	0.3341	0.4720
Some college	0.2771	0.4478	0.2805	0.4495
Bachelor's degree or higher	0.2063	0.4049	0.2951	0.4564
White, non-Hispanic	0.7274	0.4455	0.8207	0.3838
Black, non-Hispanic	0.1276	0.3338	0.0805	0.2722
Other, non-Hispanic	0.0510	0.2202	0.0537	0.2255
Hispanic	0.0939	0.2919	0.0451	0.2077
2 or more races, non-Hispanic	0.0133	0.1145	0.0329	0.1786
Less than $25,000	0.2996	0.4584	0.2183	0.4133
$25,000–$39,999	0.1870	0.3901	0.1780	0.3828
$40,000–$74,999	0.1599	0.3667	0.1780	0.3828
$75,000–$99,999	0.2183	0.4133	0.2610	0.4394
Greater than $100,000	0.1352	0.3422	0.1646	0.3711
Married	0.4994	0.5003	0.5890	0.4923
Not married	0.5006	0.5003	0.4110	0.4923
Metropolitan	0.8147	0.3888	0.8146	0.3888
Northeast	0.2039	0.4031	0.2085	0.4065
Midwest	0.2345	0.4239	0.2415	0.4282
South	0.3596	0.4802	0.3476	0.4765
West	0.2021	0.4018	0.2024	0.4021
Employed	0.4212	0.4940	0.3951	0.4892
Unemployed, in labor force	0.0736	0.2612	0.0439	0.2050
Not in labor force	0.5052	0.5003	0.5610	0.4966
Observations	820			

Cross-Tabulations for Consumers' Use of Mobile Phones

Table C.70. Do you own or have regular access to a mobile phone?
Percent, except as noted

Age categories	No	Yes	Total	Number of respondents	Percentage of users in category
18–29	9.7	90.3	100.0	387	22.3
30–44	8.9	91.1	100.0	583	26.6
45–59	12.9	87.1	100.0	843	26.9
60+	20.3	79.7	100.0	1,112	24.3
Number of respondents	322	2,603	2,925		100.0

Table C.71. Is your mobile phone a smartphone?
Percent, except as noted

Age categories	Refused	No	Yes	Total	Number of respondents	Percentage of users in category
18–29	0.5	15.1	84.4	100.0	355	26.5
30–44	0.2	13.8	86.0	100.0	546	32.2
45–59	0.3	33.0	66.6	100.0	757	25.3
60+	0.2	53.3	46.5	100.0	945	15.9
Number of respondents	8	820	1775	2,603		100.0

Table C.72. Do you own or have regular access to a mobile phone?
Percent, except as noted

Education	No	Yes	Total	Number of respondents	Percentage of users in category
Less than high school	25.6	74.4	100.0	189	10.6
High school	16.9	83.1	100.0	803	28.4
Some college	11.0	89.0	100.0	839	29.5
Bachelor's degree or higher	6.3	93.7	100.0	1,094	31.6
Number of respondents	322	2,603	2,925		100.0

Table C.73. Is your mobile phone a smartphone?
Percent, except as noted

Education	Refused	No	Yes	Total	Number of respondents	Percentage of users in category
Less than high school	0.0	48.0	52.0	100.0	144	7.8
High school	0.2	34.6	65.2	100.0	682	26.1
Some college	0.1	27.1	72.8	100.0	754	30.2
Bachelor's degree or higher	0.6	18.8	80.5	100.0	1,023	35.9
Number of respondents	8	820	1775	2,603		100.0

Table C.74. Do you own or have regular access to a mobile phone?
Percent, except as noted

Race/ethnicity	No	Yes	Total	Number of respondents	Percentage of users in category
White, non-Hispanic	11.7	88.3	100.0	2,242	66.6
Black, non-Hispanic	17.4	82.6	100.0	234	11.0
Other, non-Hispanic	14.4	85.6	100.0	115	6.4
Hispanic	14.7	85.3	100.0	248	14.9
2+ races, non-Hispanic	26.7	73.3	100.0	86	1.1
Number of respondents	**322**	**2,603**	**2,925**		**100.0**

Table C.75. Is your mobile phone a smartphone?
Percent, except as noted

Race/ethnicity	Refused	No	Yes	Total	Number of respondents	Percentage of users in category
White, non-Hispanic	0.4	31.5	68.1	100.0	2,010	64.0
Black, non-Hispanic	0.0	33.6	66.4	100.0	201	10.3
Other, non-Hispanic	0.0	17.0	83.0	100.0	101	7.5
Hispanic	0.0	18.2	81.8	100.0	216	17.2
2+ races, non-Hispanic	0.0	35.5	64.5	100.0	75	1.0
Number of respondents	**8**	**820**	**1,775**	**2,603**		**100.0**

Table C.76. Do you own or have regular access to a mobile phone?
Percent, except as noted

Income group	No	Yes	Total	Number of respondents	Percentage of users in category
Less than $25,000	26.2	73.8	100.0	465	18.4
$25,000–$39,999	15.6	84.4	100.0	409	15.0
$40,000–$74,999	10.7	89.3	100.0	494	17.0
$75,000–$99,999	9.3	90.7	100.0	742	24.1
Greater than $100,000	4.9	95.1	100.0	815	25.6
Number of respondents	**322**	**2,603**	**2,925**		**100.0**

Table C.77. Is your mobile phone a smartphone?
Percent, except as noted

Income group	Refused	No	Yes	Total	Number of respondents	Percentage of users in category
Less than $25,000	0.0	47.0	53.0	100.0	351	13.8
$25,000–$39,999	0.3	36.0	63.7	100.0	351	13.5
$40,000–$74,999	0.2	27.2	72.6	100.0	440	17.4
$75,000–$99,999	0.6	26.1	73.3	100.0	689	24.9
Greater than $100,000	0.2	15.3	84.5	100.0	772	30.5
Number of respondents	**8**	**820**	**1775**	**2,603**		**100.0**

Cross-Tabulations for Consumers' Use of Mobile Banking and Mobile Payments

C.78.a. Cross-tabulations for consumers' use of mobile banking by age, race, gender, education, and income: Smartphone users
Percent, except as noted

Use of mobile banking in past 12 months	Refused	No	Yes	Total	Number of respondents	Percentage of users in category
Age categories						
18–29	0.2	33.4	66.4	100.0	260	31.2
30–44	1.8	38.5	59.8	100.0	437	36.9
45–59	1.0	53.5	45.5	100.0	518	23.4
60+	1.1	73.1	25.7	100.0	457	8.5
Number of respondents	15	859	798	1,672		100.0
Race/ethnicity						
White, non-Hispanic	0.8	51.2	48.0	100.0	1,282	61.8
Black, non-Hispanic	0.8	43.3	55.8	100.0	117	10.1
Other, non-Hispanic	1.8	43.2	55.0	100.0	81	8.3
Hispanic	2.1	34.3	63.6	100.0	149	18.6
2+ races, non-Hispanic	0.0	38.8	61.2	100.0	43	1.1
Number of respondents	15	859	798	1,672		100.0
Gender						
Female	1.7	46.7	51.6	100.0	797	51.0
Male	0.4	47.6	52.0	100.0	875	49.0
Number of respondents	15	859	798	1,672		100.0
Education						
Less than high school	2.9	55.0	42.2	100.0	53	5.0
High school	0.1	56.3	43.6	100.0	367	20.9
Some college	1.5	42.5	56.0	100.0	492	33.3
Bachelor's degree or higher	1.1	43.8	55.2	100.0	760	40.9
Number of respondents	15	859	798	1,672		100.0
Income group						
Less than $25,000	1.3	40.9	57.8	100.0	138	12.2
$25,000–$39,999	0.5	52.2	47.3	100.0	188	12.1
$40,000–$74,999	0.7	42.0	57.3	100.0	279	20.1
$75,000–$99,999	1.1	47.6	51.3	100.0	453	25.4
Greater than $100,000	1.3	49.8	48.8	100.0	614	30.2
Number of respondents	15	859	798	1,672		100.0

C.78.b. Cross-tabulations for consumers' use of mobile payments by age, race, gender, education, and income: Smartphone users
Percent, except as noted

Use of mobile payments in past 12 months	Refused	No	Yes	Total	Number of respondents	Percentage of users in category
Age categories						
18–29	0.6	61.8	37.6	100.0	303	35.1
30–44	1.4	64.0	34.6	100.0	469	39.3
45–59	0.4	78.8	20.8	100.0	536	18.5
60+	0.1	87.3	12.6	100.0	467	7.1
Number of respondents	7	1,340	428	1,775		100.0
Race/ethnicity						
White, non-Hispanic	0.2	75.9	23.9	100.0	1,329	53.8
Black, non-Hispanic	0.0	58.3	41.7	100.0	135	15.1
Other, non-Hispanic	2.0	73.5	24.6	100.0	84	6.5
Hispanic	2.5	58.8	38.6	100.0	179	23.4
2+ races, non-Hispanic	0.0	65.0	35.0	100.0	48	1.2
Number of respondents	7	1,340	428	1,775		100.0
Gender						
Female	0.8	68.9	30.3	100.0	849	54.8
Male	0.6	73.0	26.4	100.0	926	45.2
Number of respondents	7	1,340	428	1,775		100.0
Education						
Less than high school	2.6	72.7	24.7	100.0	70	6.8
High school	0.6	74.8	24.5	100.0	406	22.6
Some college	0.7	67.7	31.5	100.0	523	33.6
Bachelor's degree or higher	0.4	70.3	29.4	100.0	776	37.1
Number of respondents	7	1,340	428	1,775		100.0
Income group						
Less than $25,000	1.5	65.0	33.6	100.0	172	16.3
$25,000–$39,999	0.5	67.8	31.8	100.0	204	15.1
$40,000–$74,999	0.9	69.3	29.8	100.0	292	18.2
$75,000–$99,999	0.0	70.8	29.2	100.0	472	25.6
Greater than $100,000	0.9	75.9	23.2	100.0	635	24.9
Number of respondents	7	1,340	428	1,775		100.0